The Commitment
to Holiness

The Commitment to Holiness

by Kenneth E. Jones
Author of *The Word of God*

COMMITMENT TO HOLINESS
BY KENNETH E. JONES

ISBN: 978-1-60416-728-3

Reformation Publishers
242 University Drive
Prestonsburg, Kentucky 41653
1-800-765-2464
rpublisher@aol.com

Printed in the United States of America

Contents

Dedicated
To all the students who have
sharpened my thinking on this
subject by their questions and
reactions.

Preface

The concept of holiness has been neglected for too long. This neglect for the last quarter-century has, I think, been caused partly by some of the extreme concepts of holiness that had come to be all too common in certain circles. A second reason is that some illustrations of entire sanctification had been pressed so far that they taught an unrealistic view of holiness. As a result, preachers felt they had to make a choice between preaching what they could neither support scripturally nor live themselves and ceasing to preach holiness altogether. Many took the latter course and sorrowfully laid the doctrine of holiness on the shelf.

Let me explain this by relating my personal quest for a biblical concept of holiness. My earliest memories are of the preaching of holiness. My father, mother, and grandmother were all ordained Church of God preachers. Dad did not ride any theological hobby-horse, but two of his favorite topics were God's church and holiness. So I have heard holiness preached from my beginning.

I also was able to hear a large number of preachers expound on the subject. We went to every camp meeting within reach, and every minister's meeting as well. And there was the steady stream of evangelists and guest preachers who preached in our church and who usually stayed in our home.

I was a most interested eavesdropper on the long conversations dad often had with these preachers on holiness, as well as other biblical topics. I soon began to notice that although dad was very strict in his personal life, he was never as extreme in his teaching as some of these other preachers. He was quick to point out the inconsistencies in their teaching and to point out that no one could live what some of them taught. I heard some say, for example, that no sanctified person could ever feel hurt at some slighting remark or insult. I even heard it preached that if one were really sanctified, he or she could never feel discouraged, doubtful, or sad. It was not hard for me to see that some who said such things were themselves discouraged at times and at times felt sad. My parents helped me see that such preachers were simply confused. Otherwise I might have given up the whole idea myself.

In spite of the poverty of those days, dad bought almost every book published by the Gospel Trumpet Company (later Warner Press). And by the time I was eight I was reading all of them as he got them. So I read F. G. Smith's *What the Bible Teaches*, R. R. Byrum's *Christian Theology*, and Allison F. Bernard's *Plain Paths to the Land of Promise, or Sanctification Made Clear*.

At Anderson College, I was privileged to study with Earl Martin and C. E. Brown, both of whom were a great help to me, although at times I resisted what they tried to teach me. While I was in graduate school, C. E. Brown's most helpful book was published, *The Meaning of Sanctification*. This book has been widely used in colleges and seminaries and rightly so. A widely known holiness theologian told me twenty years later that it was the greatest book on the subject ever written. I learned much from it but still had some questions I could not answer.

In the years that followed I studied all the relevant passages in the original languages and read all I could find on the subject. Out of the host of books that helped me in my search for understanding of holiness, two more deserve special mention: first, George Allen Turner, *The Vision Which*

Transforms: Is Christian Perfection Scriptural? (1964, Beacon Hill Press). This was a revision of an earlier work with a different title and both were based on his doctoral dissertation. It is a thorough study of the biblical basis of holiness as expounded by John Wesley. The other is Mildred Bangs Wynkoop, *A Theology of Love, the Dynamic of Wesleyanism* (1972, Beacon Hill Press). This ground-breaking study of holiness came on the scene at the right time to encourage me in some of the convictions I had been developing and had a tremendous impact on my thinking.

A host of other books and people have helped me come to the present point in my understanding of holiness. I mention these few only because the reader has a right to know something of the way in which I have come to the ideas expressed in this book of mine.

As can been seen, I have learned from a variety of people from different holiness groups, as well as from preachers and theologians in the Church of God reformation. But, like a true child of this reformation, I have sought everywhere for truth and tested it all by its agreement with the Bible. I want to be biblical in both life and thought. I have written for the Church of God reformation movement, though I would be unhappy if it did not reach out to help others also. My point is that I want to be a blessing to the group in which I have labored for more than fifty years as a preacher and teacher.

While many have contributed to my thinking on this subject, I alone am responsible for what is said here. I pray that it will help you and never cause a problem. May God continue to guide both you and me in our great personal adventure of holiness.

Chapter 1:
The Adventure of Holiness

By faith Abraham obeyed when he was called to go out to a place which he was to receive as an inheritance; and he went out, not knowing where he was to go (Heb. 11:8).

Webster defines adventure as "a venture—a risk." To attempt an adventure means attempting a feat even though you know danger may be involved and even though you do not know what all may happen. It involves the excitement of the unknown.

So we see that when Abraham left Ur, he was beginning a great adventure. He did not know where he was going, except that God wanted him to go. He did not know all the things that would befall him on the journey or at the end of it. He did not know what kind of dangers might lie ahead or what troubles he might meet on the way. But by faith in God he was willing to take the risks involved because he wanted to please God. He was determined to do anything in his power to please God.

In leaving his homeland to follow the guidance of God, Abraham was taking the risk that others would think he was most foolish. And what if his journey ended in total failure and he decided that he had made a fool of himself? How could he be sure that God was really asking this of him?

What if there was no such God after all, and he found he had gone on a wild chase after empty bubbles? Surely he thought of such a possibility. But his quiet confidence in God and God's ability to lead him caused him to go.

Adventure Involves Danger

Every real adventure involves some risk. In fact the risk is what makes it a real adventure, rather than a casual experience. From the time he left Ur Abraham's life was an adventure that was filled with unknown dangers. The trip itself was along a well-traveled trade route from Ur to Egypt. Others had made most of this trip before him. But even though the road was there, he did not know how far or just where God would lead him. So he no doubt left with may questions in his mind. I am sure God wants me to start, but will I know just where to go? Am I sure I will know when and where to stop? Will God ever speak to me again? If he does, will I understand just what it is he wants me to do?

God had not told Abraham the end from the beginning. He simply told Abraham to go—to start. He did not tell him where to go, how to get there, or how to know when he was there. He simply said, "I will show you."

God had not told Abraham what sorts of dangers he would face along the way. There were dangers in travel then as there are now. Thieves might try to take all he had. In strange countries he might have to fight for his life and the lives of those with him. A variety of calamities might befall him and his flocks of sheep. Wild animals might kill them, or they might die of disease, starvation, or thirst.

There were troubles he could have with the people who were going with them. What if some of them came to hate his leadership and tried to get rid of him? What if he had trouble keeping them from fighting one another or quarreling so as to ruin the trip? When they got to the end of the journey, what if they did not find any suitable place to live?

Such questions could have made Abraham feel that the whole venture was too risky. He would then have decided to keep his vision to himself and stay at home where it was safer. But he did not. He was willing to venture out on the journey to an unknown homeland because he was sure God would go with him. We are not told how he came to this assurance and faith in God. But he did. So he went.

Abraham's Faith Was in God

Abraham's faith was not mere faith in his own ability as an explorer. It was not confidence in his own leadership. It was not faith in himself at all, but it was faith in God.

Yet we get to the heart of the matter only when we realize also that the faith of Abraham was not faith in a good map. "He went out, not knowing where he was to go." God did not give him a map at all, but said, "I will show you." This meant to Abraham that God himself would go with him on the whole trip. God would show him where and when to go. God would be his helper on the trip in all the dangers he might have to face.

The story is told of a man going through a Central American jungle with a native guide. They came to a place where no way could be seen through the dense jungle. As he looked at the impenetrable jungle ahead, he could see no path at all and wondered if they were already lost. He asked the guide, "Where is the path? How can we know where to go?" The guide merely started forward again, and said, "I am the path. Come with me." This is what Jesus did when he said to Thomas, "I am the way."

But remember that Abraham lived long before Thomas and had never had the experience of talking face to face with his Lord in that way. He was pioneering in an unknown way. He was leaving the gods of his neighbors and going out to seek to follow his God, who had promised to go with him. His faith in God gave him confidence.

How did Abraham come to have such faith in God when he lived in a pagan, polytheistic culture? We can speculate about visions, dreams, and such, but the fact is that we do not know. We are told a little about some of the ways God appeared to him later, but not about the first messages and how he felt so sure of God's presence and guidance.

3

Actually, it does not matter to us. Each of us has to come to a personal knowledge of God in his or her own way. We must not seek too inquisitively about how others come to know God in person. We ourselves must know him. God will help us to know him if we seek after him. To one person, he reveals himself in a dream. To another, in a vision. To another in some indescribable way. One may simply come to an assurance of God's presence and blessing without ever being able to say how it came about. The only important thing is to know God. How it comes about is not important, since God in his wisdom knows how to make himself known to each of us. He knows us, and he knows exactly how to make himself known to each of us.

Holiness Is an Adventure

Holiness is an adventure because it means going through life with God. Holiness means living under God's direction, belonging only to God, being guided by the Holy Spirit, and learning from the God who made us.

It is all too common for us to think of holiness as following a rule-book, and never breaking any of the written rules. If this is what holiness is, then it can be very difficult because we might forget one of the rules, or might not ever learn them all. We can then go through life feeling that some saint somewhere might possibly rise to the achievement of holiness, but not any of us ordinary mortals. Or we can go through life defeated because we know of rules we have broken or of times when we have forgotten our high resolves. To think of holiness as a set of rules to keep is to invite certain defeat.

I invite you instead to think of holiness as a personal walk through life with a personal God. Holiness then is no longer memorizing a set of rules that seems unending. Holiness is following our living Lord, by his grace and help.

This does not mean there are no written guidelines for living, and no rules. This does not mean, for instance, that the Ten Commandments are no longer valid guides. But in following God personally, we go far beyond the rules. Rules are primarily negative. Do not kill. Do not steal. Holiness is positive guidance.

In the Sermon on the Mount, Jesus pointed the way to go beyond the Ten Commandments. First he insisted that he had not come to destroy the Law, but to fulfill it. Then he gave some illustrations. He said:

> You have heard that it was said to the men of old, "You shall not kill; and whoever kills shall be liable to judgment." But I say to you that every one who is angry with his brother shall be liable to judgment; whoever insults his brother shall be liable to the council, and whoever says, "You fool!" shall be liable to the hell of fire (Matt. 5:21-23).

He did the same kind of thing with the other illustrations he used. A careful study of the whole chapter shows that Jesus was not giving a new set of rules for living that he would substitute for the Ten Commandments. Instead, he was saying that we must go beyond the rules and seek to love both God and others as God loves them. In fact, he closes this chapter with the idea that we must love everybody, as God does, and not just love those who love us.

It is not that the Ten Commandments are not good, or that they were not given by God. They were inspired by God. But they were only a beginning point for pleasing God. They were necessary first steps toward fellowship with God who in Christ Jesus lifts you higher and higher above the first steps you took to get to him.

Personal Adventure

Now maybe we are ready to see the true nature of the adventure of holiness. It is walking by the moment-to-moment guidance of the Holy Spirit. We do not know the way ahead, but we know the Guide who will go with us every step of the way. We do not know what we will have to face, or when we will have to face it. We do not know where God will lead us in the future or what he will lead us to do. But we are happy to go anywhere, so long as he will go with us.

5

Like Abraham, we go out, not knowing where we are going. But like him, we have the assurance that God will go with us and be our daily guide. We have no map of our personal lives. God has not even promised to tell us ahead of time what we will be doing later on. But God has promised that he will never forsake us. He will be with us in all that we do if we keep on making him welcome in our hearts and in our lives.

There is risk in living in this way. Some find it harder than others to take this risk. They like to have everything well planned in their own minds. They cannot feel good if they do not know clearly just what they will be doing in the future, and how and when they will be doing it. But this life of holiness has to be a life of steady faith. We not only must have faith to begin the life with God, but faith must not falter any day or moment. We must take each step believing firmly that God will direct us to the next step. The faith that is needed is not faith in our own plans or faith in our own understanding of God's plans; but it must be faith in God. We need faith in God's leadership. And we need faith that God will give us grace and strength to know and follow his leadership.

Holiness, then, is personal fellowship with a personal God. We love him because we know that he first loved us. We do not merely know *of* him; we know him. We have not merely read the inspired Word about him; we have come to know him for ourselves. Through the death of Christ on the cross for us, we have come to know the assurance of sins forgiven. Then we have given our saved selves wholly to God. We have accepted the gift of the Holy Spirit to guide us moment by moment throughout the rest of our lives on earth and to receive us into our eternal home. We have not insisted on a detailed map of the whole journey but are willing to go with him wherever he may lead us, so long as he will not forsake us.

So the adventure of holiness is the thrill of facing the unknown future with a sure confidence in the power and guidance of the Holy Spirit.

An Imperative Adventure

It is important for us to remember that this adventure of holiness is not our own invention and not a humanly devised concept. God has commanded us to live holy lives in this way. He commands us to follow him in faith. He requires us to forsake everything that would displease him or that would lead us in wrong ways, and to go out into the unknown future with him.

God has commanded us to seek to live lives, by his grace and power, which will please him in every way. None of us can do this on our own power or in our own wisdom. We are weak and we are ignorant. But Jesus died to save us from sin so that we can truly please God.

We shall be looking at some of the biblical commands to holiness and will be studying what it means to please God in all that we do. We will be seeking to understand how it is possible that fallible, weak, ignorant human beings can hope to please the infinite God. But what we need to understand for the moment is that this is possible, and that God has commanded it. What God commands, he gives power to do—if we will submit to learn and do his will.

Holiness Is Love

This, too, we will study in more depth, but for now we may be content to say it. When John Wesley, who pioneered the modern revival of scriptural holiness, tried to explain what holiness means, he always insisted that holiness is love for God and godly love for others. In this he was simply following the clearest New Testament teachings. Our love for God, in response to his love for us, makes us willing and even eager to forsake all else and follow God wherever he may lead. Our love for God makes us want to do whatever will please him and to go wherever he chooses for us to go. Our love for him who saved us from sin makes us willing even to suffer, if need be, to do his will. Our love for God makes this life of holiness a life of joyous adventure. Following him is not hard but is instead the most pleasant and rewarding life we can imagine. There is nothing else we would choose to do—nothing else we want to do. In our love for him we resist every temptation that may come to forsake his way. Love for God makes all life a thrilling adventure— the adventure of holiness!

Chapter 2:
God Is Holy

Our human understanding of the nature of holiness comes from God. Our very understanding that holiness exists has been revealed by God, and would not be known otherwise.

We know about holiness only because God declares that he is holy. This revelation of God's holiness comes to us in our day through the Bible, which records what God has revealed to various persons in many ways before, during, and after the life of Christ on earth. After the sin of the first couple, God began the long, slow process of revealing to human beings all that we need to know of his own nature, the sinfulness of sin, and the plan for the salvation of humankind from sin. This is why the special revelation of God's will in the Bible came to an end with the death of those who knew Jesus in his life on earth. The plan of salvation was then finished, and the Good News was ready to be proclaimed to all the earth.

When God spoke to Moses at the burning bush, he said to him, "Do not come near; put off your shoes from your feet, for the place on which you are standing is holy ground" (Exod. 3:5).

It would be difficult for us to overemphasize the impor-

9

tance of this event in the life of Moses. In this first clear vision of God, Moses was led to see the holiness of God. He was to consider the very ground sacred because he was in the presence of the holy God who created all that is. From this time on, Moses could not think of God apart from holiness. A little later, when Moses had led the people through the Red Sea by means of God's miraculous action, he led the people in singing a song of deliverance. He sang, "Who is like thee, O Lord, among the gods: who is like thee, majestic in holiness, terrible in glorious deeds, doing wonders?" (Exod. 15:11).

The vision of God as holy became a ruling force in the thought of Moses about God. It controlled what he said to the people about God. When they came to the mountain where he had first had this encounter with God, he told the people to cleanse themselves because God was about to appear to them. They were not to come casually into the presence of God, but must take three days to prepare themselves (Exod. 19:10-13). Further, they must be careful not to touch the mountain itself, for it was holy to the Lord. God used this method of beginning to teach the people that the Lord God of heaven and earth is not to be taken lightly. He is holy, awe-inspiring, powerful, loving, but demanding.

The holiness of God was given as the chief reason for the holiness of God's people. "And you shall be to me a kingdom of priests and a holy nation" (Exod. 19:6). "You shall be holy to me; for I the Lord am holy, and have separated you from the peoples, that you should be mine" (Lev. 20:26). "You shall be holy; for I the Lord your God am holy" (Lev. 19:2).

When Isaiah had his great vision of God in the temple, the point of the message he received was the holiness of God. He says:

In the year that King Uzziah died I saw the Lord sitting upon a throne, high and lifted up; and his train filled the temple. Above him stood the seraphim. . . . And one called to another and said: "Holy, holy, holy is the Lord of hosts; the whole earth is full of his glory" (Isa. 6:1-3).

This vision so impressed Isaiah with the holiness of God that he immediately felt himself to be unclean and unfit even to speak of God. But God cleansed him and sent him to preach the divine message to the people. Isaiah liked to call God "the Holy One of Israel" as a result of this vision. And his message was that if human beings are to please a holy God, they must be clean and righteous themselves.

The fact is that the whole Old Testament is dominated by the concept of the holiness of God. It is confirmed in the New Testament but is not often mentioned. Like the idea of the oneness of God, this had been so strongly set forth in the Old Testament that little had to be said of it in the New.

If we are ever to be holy ourselves, we must have some vision of the holiness of God. It is not at all necessary that we have a vision in the sense that Isaiah did, for that is extremely rare. But our spiritual eyes must be opened to the glory and holiness of God. We must come to see him not as "the man upstairs" or a "pal" who is on our own level, but as the God of the universe, the Creator of all things. We know that he loves us, but we must not forget who it is who loves us. He is our Father, but we must always remember that he is our "Father in heaven." He is our Savior, but he is also still our judge.

Seeing the holiness of God will show us our own sinfulness and need for cleansing. This is primarily true as we come to know God's holiness for the first time. Then, like Isaiah, we can admit our need for cleansing and find that God freely provides it. If we submit ourselves to God, it is his will to make us clean and holy so that we can live so as to please him more and more.

Meaning of God's Holiness

Holiness is difficult to define precisely. The fact is that its meaning as applied to God is not exactly the same as when applied to human beings or to things. This is true because God alone is holy in and of himself. He alone is holy in his very being. If we are considered holy, our holiness is only in a relative sense, and it expresses our relationship with God. That is, our holiness is a result of God's love for us and grace to us. It means first of all that we belong to him in a special sense—because he is willing to claim us as his own special people. We can see this more clearly by looking first at the two major aspects of God's holiness, as revealed in the Bible.

Awe-Inspiring Transcendence

God's transcendence means first of all that God is not a part of the universe. No matter where we go in the whole universe, we could never invade God's presence; God is not part of the universe that he has made.

When John Glenn made that first space trip, he really did not go very high, but he went high enough to make some good people feel uneasily that he was invading God's heaven and might bring punishment on humanity! But even walking on the moon or on a distant planet, one is no nearer God and no farther from God than on the earth and deep in a mine. God is not a part of the universe at all, but is always Something Other than any thing. He is always above and beyond.

Whenever God reveals himself, he inspires awe and reverence in the one to whom he reveals himself. Moses put off his shoes from his feet in reverence. Isaiah felt his own total inadequacy. Job realized in the presence of God that all his speeches had been make in ignorance (Job 40:3-5). The Israelites at the foot of Mount Sinai felt they could not bear the presence of God and begged Moses to listen for them and tell them what God had said (Exod. 20:18-21).

God is not to be approached casually. In Christ we can approach God's throne confidently in prayer. "Let us then with confidence draw near to the throne of grace, that we may receive mercy and find grace to help in time of need" (Heb. 4:16). But this is only because God himself graciously sent his Son to show us the way, and to make it possible.

We must never forget that God is not on our level. He is not the "man upstairs" or a heavenly Santa Claus. He is not controlled by our prayers, and our prayers must never sound like orders. Even Jesus prayed, "My Father . . . not as I will, but as thou wilt" (Matt. 26:39).

But we cannot speak of the transcendence of God without balancing it with discussion of his *immanence*. God does transcend all creation, but he is also present in every corner of it. He is not a part of the universe, yet there is no place in it where God is not. As the psalmist said in his own way, there is no place one can go where God is not there. (See Psalms 139:7-12.) The sinner may not like this, but to the Christian it is a wonderful comfort.

The basic idea in this aspect of God's holiness is that God is utterly different from human beings and different from any part of the creation. He is not separated from the universe, but he is different from it. He is not any part of it.

In all of this we are coming close to saying that the basic idea of holiness is *separation*. And this is true when the word is applied to God. But it is not the whole truth when the word is applied to things or to people. In such cases, *holy* means "separate to God," "belonging to God alone," and anyone or anything belonging to God in any special sense must have characteristics that are pleasing to him. We will study this more thoroughly in the next chapter.

The Brightness of His Glory

A second aspect of God's holiness is the brightness of his glory. The post-biblical word *shekinah* is not found in the Bible, but it is often now used for this shining glory of God. It is implied in Isaiah 60:2, "For behold, darkness shall cover the earth, and thick darkness the peoples; but the LORD will arise upon you, and his glory will be seen upon you." His unapproachable brightness is referred to also in Exodus 24:17, where it is said that "the glory of the LORD was like a devouring fire on the top of the mountain."

The full effect of this brightness of God is seen at the dedi-

13

cation of the tabernacle at Sinai and of the temple of Solomon in Jerusalem. When the tabernacle was completed and dedicated, we are told:

> Then the cloud covered the tent of meeting, and the glory of the LORD filled the tabernacle. And Moses was not able to enter the tent of meeting, because the cloud abode upon it, and the glory of the LORD filled the tabernacle (Exod. 40:34).

The point that is stressed here is that the ineffable glory of God keeps him from being approached too closely. The same cloud that revealed his presence also kept everyone at a certain distance. This was a cloud by day and a pillar of fire by night (Exod. 13:21-22; Num. 9:15). This same cloud was seen on Mount Sinai while Moses was there with God (Exod. 24:15-16). And we remember that God first appeared to Moses in a fiery bush (Exod. 3:3-6). The fire represents the brightness of the glory and holiness of God, and the cloud form serves as a screen between us and God, since the true glory of God can never be seen by human eyes. The holiness of God is such that it cannot be fully comprehended or directly experienced by human beings. As the Philistines asked after their experiences with the ark of the covenant, "Who is able to stand before the LORD, this holy God?" (1 Sam. 6:20).

God's Absolute Purity

God is absolutely perfect in purity, righteousness, justice, mercy, and love. These five attributes make up his moral perfection.

1. *God's absolute purity.* As John put it, "God is light and in him is no darkness at all" (1 John 1:5). This kind of purity is beyond our comprehension as human beings, as are all absolute perfections. Only by the mercy of God can we be called pure by God. His cleansing purifies us, as we know, but we have continual need of the mercy of God to forgive our shortcomings and failures, and to keep on accepting us. God is absolute purity of will and action.

The Old Testament prophet Habakkuk said that God is "of purer eyes than to behold evil" (Hab. 1:13). This cannot mean that God is so pure that he cannot see evil in human beings, but rather that God cannot look upon evil with approval. We tend to gaze at those things that we approve, and God can never approve evil. God is pure.

2. *God's absolute righteousness.* God never commits sin, not because God is restrained by some power other than himself, but because it is his nature to be righteous. God is the very source of our understanding of what righteousness is. He is the source of our goodness, and of our understanding of what is good. God is absolutely good and can never be otherwise.

The fact that *holiness* and *righteousness* have nearly the same meaning in English is a tribute to the Old Testament prophets, who taught so clearly that right living is essential if we are to know the holy God. It is not enough to call ourselves a holy people; we must be right in all our living. Those prophets spelled out for the people just what standards of righteousness they must know and practice in order to be God's holy people. So the word *holy* is misunderstood if we do not include *righteousness* in its concept.

3. *God's absolute justice.* God's justice means that he must punish sin and the sinner. God cannot approve or love sin, no matter how much he loves the sinner. His justice is absolute, not the relative justice of human beings. Since it is coupled with his perfect knowledge, he never makes a mistake in his judgment of a person.

4. *God's absolute mercy.* God's justice is perfectly balanced by his mercy. Justice without mercy would be intolerable to all of the human race. And mercy without justice would open the door to anarchy and would not really be merciful at all. So in God justice and mercy are perfectly balanced. This is why God can condemn sin so severely and yet show mercy to the repentant sinner. The psalmist was really describing the mercy of God when he said:

As a father pities his children,
so the Lord pities those who fear him.

15

For he knows our frame;
he remembers that we are dust (Ps. 103:13, 14).

This mercy of God is not something that we deserve, or it would not truly be mercy. It is the unmerited favor of God, which is so wonderful simply because it is totally undeserved. Jesus stressed this when he said, "So you also, when you have done all that is commanded you, say 'We are unworthy servants; we have only done what was our duty' " (Luke 17:10).

5. *God's perfect love.* It is God's love for us that teaches us what love is and causes us to love him. Our love for him is no wonderful thing, but is only the proper response to God's love for us. "We love, because he first loved us" (1 John 4:19).

God loved us when we were totally unlovely and were as yet incapable of returning love to him. This is the marvel of God's love for us. God loves us, not because of what we are, but because of who he is. God is love.

A problem with saying that God is love, is that the word *love* has been abused in the last two or three decades. It has come to mean almost anything, so that it means almost nothing to many people. God's love is not to be compared with what we often call love. For us, love may be a refined self-interest or a warm, soft feeling. But we can never understand the love of God unless we get far beyond such concepts and realize that we do not know all about love. If this is all love is, we will stumble over the statements that "God is love," and "our God is a consuming fire."

To understand what the Bible says about the nature of God's love, we need to see it revealed in the death of Christ on the cross. There Jesus showed us divine love. He did not have to die, and did not even have to come into the world. He did it because of his great love for us. He chose to die, not because of some martyr complex, but because he loves us and wants us to love him.

We will never understand the Bible teaching about love if we try to reason from human love to God's love. So long as we try to understand what it means for human beings to love and then say that God's love is like that, we cannot understand what the Bible is saying. We *must* begin at the cross of Christ. When we do this, we can see some important aspects of God's love: (a) God's love for us is not based on anything in us, but only on God's nature. (b) It is not mixed with any selfishness or self-concern. (c) It is holy love. (d) So God loves sinners without approving them or their actions. (e) God loves so deeply that he must despise the sin that destroys us. (f) God's love is just and must punish sin. (g) God's love is not wishy-washy emotion. (h) Love seeks the good of all. (i) God's love is self-giving. (j) God's love never fails, but is eternal. (k) God's love seeks our ultimate good, not temporary benefits. (l) God's love seeks our eternal salvation.

So we can see the contrast between God's holy love and the various emotions that we can call human love. Thus God's love is one important aspect of his holiness and along with his purity, righteousness, justice, and mercy, makes up the moral purity of God's holiness.

Summary

We have been trying to understand something of the nature and meaning of the holiness of God, because that is the starting point for understanding the biblical idea of holiness. Since the Bible is so insistent that God is holy, we need to know what the term means.

As we have seen, the holiness of God has three major aspects: his transcendence, his shining glory, and his moral purity. The last we have divided into his purity, righteousness, justice, mercy, and love. This helps us to understand just what is meant by God's moral purity.

In the next chapter we shall look at the word *holy* as it is applied to things and to human beings. In doing so we shall see that it cannot mean the same as when applied to God, but our understanding of God's holiness helps us to see what the Bible means in the other cases.

Chapter 3:
Be Ye Holy

For I am the Lord your God; consecrate yourselves therefore, and be holy, for I am holy. . . . You shall therefore be holy, for I am holy (Lev. 11:44, 45).

But as he who called you is holy, be holy yourselves in all your conduct; since it is written, "You shall be holy, for I am holy" (1 Pet. 1:15-16).

Strive for peace . . . , and for the holiness without which no one will see the Lord (Heb. 12:14).

These passages make clear the fact that God's word commands us to be holy. Yet we have seen that the holiness of God consists of his utter transcendence, his shining glory, and his perfect moral purity. The first two of these are totally unique to God, and the third seems out of reach of human beings. So how is it possible for human beings to be holy?

The problem is so great that the majority simply say that human holiness is impossible, at least in this life. They conclude that sin is the inevitable malady of all who live on this earth and they hope that death will somehow end the reign of death and make it possible for us to live with victory in heaven. But if this is so, why does God so insistently tell

19

us to be holy? Is it just to tantalize us? Or is it to make us all the more conscious of our guilt and sin from which we cannot escape? If so, surely we Christians are doomed to be miserable all our lives. Yet this is not at all what the New Testament describes as the lot of Christians. We are not constantly living under condemnation. Paul rejoiced to declare, "There is therefore now no condemnation for those who are in Christ Jesus. For the law of the Spirit of life in Christ Jesus has set me free from the law of sin and death" (Rom. 8:1, 2). "For sin will have no dominion over you, since you are not under law but under grace" (Rom. 6:14).

Such passages teach us clearly that something is wrong with saying that human beings cannot be holy, as God has commanded. But how is it possible for us to be like God in holiness?

Meaning of Human Holiness

Bible scholars have long sought to discern the meaning of the term *holy* by tracing its etymological origin, that is, by finding out what the root form of the word originally meant, either in Greek, Hebrew, or one of the cognate languages. The most common etymology seeks to trace the word to a root that meant "to cut" or "to separate." So it has been said that the root meaning of the word *holy* is "separation." N. H. Snaith in his book *The Distinctive Ideas of the Old Testament*, takes a definite step forward when he insists that it means "separation *to* (God)," not "separation *from*" something else.[1] However, the etymology of this word is very doubtful in any case. And recent advances in linguistics have shown that etymology is never a very sure guide to the meaning of a word.

The fact is that if we are to learn the meaning of a biblical word, we will simply have to study the Bible uses of the word very carefully.

Moses was introduced to the word when he met God at the burning bush, and God said to him, "Do not come near; put off your shoes from your feet, for the place on which you are standing is holy ground" (Exod. 3:5). So the first use

20

of the word is of a holy *place*. But this is not the important thing about the passage. The important thing is to see that *holy* is here used of an encounter with the holy God. The place was not holy of itself, but only because it was where Moses encountered God, who is holy. Moses was told to show proper respect to his maker, in this case, by taking off his shoes in God's presence. The fact that Moses was in the presence of God made the place holy.

Holy Things

Later, when Moses and the people of Israel arrived at the foot of the same mountain where Moses had met with God, he declared to them that the whole mountain was holy, and they must "sanctify themselves" to be ready to meet with God.

Then when they built the tabernacle, it was to be a representation and reminder of God's presence in the midst of the people, so the tabernacle and all that was in it were declared to be holy. None of the vessels of the tabernacle were to be used for ordinary, common purposes, but kept for use in the worship of God alone. These vessels were holy in the sense that they belonged especially to God. All things belonged to God the Creator, but these were considered holy because of their special relationship with him.

Still later, when the temple was built as a permanent sanctuary for worship, the vessels in it were all treated as holy, just as they had been in the tabernacle. Holy objects belong especially to God.

So in the whole Bible, objects are not considered to be holy in and of themselves, but because of some special relationship with God. This is derivative holiness, and only God is holy in his own nature. Some of the things that are called holy, besides the tabernacle and the vessels used in it, are the sabbath (Exod. 20:8; 35:2) the tithe (Lev. 27:30), and offerings (2 Chron. 35:13). As can be seen by a consideration of the context in each case, these things are called holy because of their special relationship with God. The day is to be regarded as holy by God's people in that it is to be dedicated to worship of God, rather than to doing ordinary pursuits. The tithe is holy because it belongs to God in a special sense, as token of the fact that all we have belongs to God. The offerings are holy for the same reason; they are dedicated to God.

In this gospel age, we do not think of material things as being holy in this special sense, because we know very well that the whole universe belongs to God. All that we have belongs to God and is holy, so we no longer feel compelled to call only certain things holy. But the Old Testament was a time of preparation for the gospel and a time of teaching. The word *law*, which was applied to the teachings of the first five books of the Bible, really translates the Hebrew word *Torah*, which means "instruction." It is not laws passed by God or people, but God's instruction of his people in the things that would enable them to understand Christ and what he was to do in the world. It was a "school master" (Gr. *paidagogus*) to lead us to Christ (Gal. 3:25), and now that Christ has come, we are no longer under that kind of guidance. But the instruction of the Old Testament is a most valuable guide to us in seeking to understand the fullness of the gospel to which it pointed.

Thus we see that the idea of things being holy because of their special use by God, or relationship to him, was a most valuable and necessary step toward understanding the deeper meanings of holiness. For these things to be holy meant that they had to be kept *separate to* God, who is holy.

Holy Persons

In the Old Testament, priests and Levites were both called *holy* (Exod. 29:1; Lev. 8:12, 30) because they had been set apart for special ministry to God. Nazarites were "holy" because they had separated themselves to God (Num. 6:5). Most important of all, the people of Israel were holy to the Lord (Exod. 19:6; cf. Lev. 20:24) because they had separated themselves unto the Lord. In every case, these people were called holy, not because they were separated *from* something, but because they were separated *to* God. It was the fact that

22

they belonged to God in some special sense, that they were holy.

In the New Testament, the Greek word *hagios* (holy) corresponds closely to the Old Testament Hebrew *qadosh*, and is used to translate it. The word is applied to God (John 17:11; Rev. 4:8; 6:10). It is regularly applied to the Spirit of God (Matt. 1:18; Acts 1:2; Rom. 5:5), so that he is normally called the Holy Spirit. It is applied to Christ (Mark 1:24; Acts 3:14; 4:3). And it is applied to the Scriptures (Rom. 1:2), the Law (Rom. 7:12), the Mount of Transfiguration (2 Pet. 1:18), and the New Jerusalem (Rev. 21:2).

But the primary use of the word *holy* in the New Testament is of the people of God, Christians, who make up the church. This characteristic use in the New Testament is distinctive and important. Christians are regularly called "saints" (*hagioi*, plural), which could be translated "holy persons." It is applied to all born-again believers in Christ, whether they are spiritually and ethically mature or not. So the word *holy* as applied to Christians does not imply that they are morally mature, but that they have started on the road that must lead to that ideal as soon as possible. We shall see more and more why this should be true, and why it is possible to call someone *holy* who does not yet measure up to the standard of Christ in many respects. Suffice it to say here that it may be compared to a baby, who is a human being, though he or she is far from physical, intellectual, and motor maturity. We must never forget that the New Testament leaves no room for holiness divorced from high ethical standards or obedience to God.

What we are saying here is so important that it must not be misunderstood. We must not get the idea that the word *holy* is so broad that it can be applied to just anyone. It is not. But the primary meaning of the word is that we belong to God in a special sense. We must live a holy life *because* we belong to God. We are not holy because of all that we have separated ourselves *from*. It is first necessary to be *separated to* the holy God. As soon as that is done, one is holy, even though one will continue to be learning all that it is necessary

23

to be separated *from.*

Holy to the Lord

To understand all this better, we need to take a closer look at the Hebrew and Greek words involved. In the Old Testament, the Hebrew word is *gadosh*. An old suggestion is that the word came from *chadash*, meaning "new," but this is not now understood to be possible. A second suggestion has been that it is related to the Babylonian *quddushu*, meaning "bright, shining." But this also would not make sense, since we have earlier uses of the word in Hebrew than in Neo-babylonian, so the suggestion is not linguistically defensible. The third suggestion is that the root is *qd*, meaning to divide or separate. Since this was first suggested by Baudissin in 1878, it has become almost universally accepted. This does not mean that it is right, and it cannot be proved, but it is the best explanation we know. It would correspond with the Greek word used in the New Testament, *hagios*, which comes from a root with the meaning "to divide or separate."

But the problem remains that the etymological history of a word does not tell us what the word is used to mean. For example, the English word *conversation* comes from two Latin words, which together mean "a turning about, a way of life." But that does not explain what a conversation is! And the story of the way in which the word has changed its meaning since coming into English does not explain what a conversation is, but only how we got the word. So it is that the history of the words *gadosh*, and *hagios* does not help us to greatly understand the idea of holiness. The only way to do that is to study the way the words are used in the Bible.

As we have seen, God is holy in a sense in which no human being can ever be. God is transcendent with shining glory, and he is absolutely perfect morally. Yet God tells us to be holy, for he is holy.

The all-important clue is seen when we notice that all the material things and persons called holy had been dedicated especially to God. The things were not to be used for ordinary purposes, but only for the place of worship, whether in the tabernacle or the temple. The objects were no longer considered ordinary or common, because they belonged to God in a special sense. In the same way, persons were considered holy, not ordinary or common, because of their special contact and relationship with God. They belonged to God. They were totally set apart for him and his service. So they were no longer common or ordinary, but holy to God.

Common, Clean, Unclean

One way to understand the meaning of a word is through a study of contrasting words and opposites. A careful study of the uses of *holy* shows that a strong contrast is drawn between objects and persons that are holy, and those that are common (Heb. chol). Objects that are common may or may not be sinful, since uncleanness is often ceremonial uncleanness alone, not ethical or moral uncleanness. A person who was ceremonially unclean for some reason was unfit to be dedicated to God or to go into sacred places until he or she did whatever forms or ceremonies were required to be cleansed. Then he or she was fit to come into sacred places or to worship. God used this concept to teach the people that worshiping God and being his people were no light matters. God will not accept anything sinful, common, or unfit. God will have only the best.

An even stronger term used in contrast with *holy* is *cherem*. This word is difficult to translate because we have no such concept in our day, though it was very common in Israel and in the neighboring nations. One of the translations of the word is *devoted*. But it does not mean simply "devoted," but "devoted to some god other than the Lord God." This could be said of a thing or a person. To be *cherem*, then, was far worse than to be *unclean*. Some objects that were *cherem* could be made clean (undevoted), and therefore made fit to dedicate to God. Gold vessels from Jericho, for instance, were *cherem* because they had been dedicated to the gods of Jericho. But gold could be purified by fire and by ceremonies and dedicated to God. They could not be used for ordinary purposes, but had to be dedicated to God (Deut. 20:10-18; Josh. 6:15-19). Objects that were *cherem* and could not be cleansed *had to be destroyed.* This is why the word *cherem* is sometimes translated "utterly destroyed" (Josh. 6:18).

If persons who were *cherem* because they served other gods, chose to serve the Lord, then they had that right to go through the ceremonies of cleansing. Then they could dedicate themselves to God and thus become holy to the Lord. If they did not so choose, they were to be destroyed. This is the background for such commands as Deuteronomy 20:10-18. It is the reason the people of Jericho and other such cities and nations were to be utterly destroyed. God was teaching the people that there was to be no compromise with idolatry or paganism. If they were to be his people they had to be utterly and permanently separate from false gods.

Let us now take a closer look at the words *clean* and *unclean* as used in the Bible. *Clean* does not mean holy, and *unclean* does not mean common. As can be seen from the chart, both clean and unclean objects or persons could be common. The thought is rather that whatever is clean is capable of being made holy, and whatever is unclean is incapable of being made holy, unless it could first be made clean. All persons could be rendered temporarily unclean by a number of things, such as touching a dead person (Num. 5:1-2; 19:11ff). Such a person could not participate in the religious ceremonies until he or she had been cleansed by the process outlined for such cleansing (Num. 19).

Some things were by nature thought of as unclean and therefore unfit for any use by God in the tabernacle. They were also unfit for human use and to be avoided. Swine, for example, were unclean, as were a whole group of birds and animals.

A person could be unclean without being sinful. This is important to know when reading that touching a dead person, for instance, made one temporarily unclean. It was not a sin to touch one who had died, but it simply rendered the person ceremonially unclean for a time and made it necessary for him or her to go through a cleansing ceremony, which included washing one's body and clothing. In the light of modern medical knowledge of transmissible diseases, that was a good rule! But the important aspect of this is that the uncleanness was ceremonial, not moral. An unclean person or thing could not be dedicated to God until cleansed.

This concept of clean and unclean was valid under the old covenant, though even in that period, many distorted the truth. This was especially true by the time of Christ. The Pharisees condemned Christ because he did not wash his hands in their special ceremonial way before eating. But Jesus explained that "not what goes into the mouth defiles a man, but what comes out of the mouth, this defiles a man" (Matt. 15:11). The disciples, having been taught the Pharisaic way all their lives, were slow to understand and asked Jesus to explain further. He said:

> Are you also still without understanding? Do you not see that whatever goes into the mouth passes into the stomach, and so passes on? But what comes out of the mouth proceeds from the heart, and this defiles a man. For out of the heart come evil thoughts, murder, adultery, fornication, theft, false witness, slander. These are what defile a man; but to eat with unwashed hands does not defile a man (Matt. 15:16-20).

It is apparent that the Pharisees were making two mistakes. They were not distinguishing between ceremonial uncleanness and dirt. And they were not distinguishing ceremonial uncleanness from sin.

In Peter's famous rooftop vision of the sheet full of clean and unclean animals, the understanding was made very clear to him that the old covenant rules of ceremonially clean and unclean were no longer necessary. They had had their valuable place in teaching the people what it means to be pleasing to God, but now that Christ has revealed the reality of true Christian holiness, we no longer need that kind of instruction. Everything that God has made, was made good and fit for proper human use. In this gospel age we must not call any persons *unclean*, meaning that they are unfit for the gospel. The good news must be preached to all, and those who accept it can be made God's own people. Sin is what defiles a person, and sin can be cleansed away by God in Christ Jesus, so that no one is inherently incapable of being made a Christian.

The old rules were not wrong. They were good and proper but were given for a temporary lesson in what it means to be pleasing to God. Later, the rules are no longer necessary. When we teach a small child not *ever* to cross the street without an adult, this is a good rule and vitally necessary to the child. But when the child is older, he or she should have learned the lesson of danger in the street, and should be capable of ignoring the rule for the rest of his or her life. In something of the same way, the Old Testament ceremonies and rituals were given to teach spiritual lessons. When the spiritual reality appeared in Christ and his death and resurrection, the old rules became unnecessary.

In the Old Testament, the fullest meaning of *holy* as applied to persons, is that they *belong especially to God*. This meaning carries over into the New Testament, but it is given a deeper spiritual meaning. In the Old Testament, the people of Israel were called holy because they were God's own people whom he had chosen for himself (Exod. 19:5-6). But this was done in an anticipatory sense. The fact is that at times God did not claim them as his own because of their sin (Hos. 1:9). In this gospel age, we know that the individual Christian must be holy, not because he or she was born into a particular nation, but because the person as an individual has accepted the spiritual cleansing offered in Christ Jesus, and has voluntarily let God make him or her holy. The Old Testament sanctification is inward and spiritual.

As to the matter of belonging to God, more needs to be said both here and later. In a sense everything in the universe belongs to God, by right of creation. He made it all, and it is his. But clearly from the first use of the word in the Bible this was not all there is to the word. All people are under the dominion of God, but not all admit it. They do not belong to God in the special sense of being his people. God does not claim them as his. This is because he has given each person some freedom of choice. We can choose whether or not we want to put ourselves under God's control and let him have his way with us. Only *persons* can be holy, then, in the New Testament sense. And persons cannot be holy in this full sense unless they themselves choose to allow God to cleanse them, break the power of sin and the devil, and be made holy to the Lord. Thus the word has a far deeper and richer meaning in the New Testament age than in the Old.

This concept of *belonging to God*, as the essence of biblical holiness, was spelled out by C. E. Brown in one of the last articles he published on the subject. It was published in a 1954 *Gospel Trumpet* (now *Vital Christianity*), titled "A New Approach to Sanctification." He pointed out that he was writing it after preaching sanctification and holiness for sixty years. (I have preached it for only fifty years.) It would be worth quoting a few lines from this excellent article:

> There is an outstanding truth of the doctrine of holiness that we have neglected for a long time. It is this: The holy thing is the thing that belongs to God. For purposes of study, this is probably the best approach to the subject. . . .
>
> Before men knew much about being pure in heart, they knew a great deal about things belonging to God. This is the road of knowledge by which men came to learn about holiness. It is the kindergarten of religious instruction. . . .
>
> The very first thing we can say about the holy man is that he belongs to God. And just as certainly we can say with the absolute assurance of stating a mathematical axiom: Every man who belongs to God is holy. . . .
>
> Let us not insist too much upon how good we are (not denying it), but let us emphasize this truth that we have only the minimum standard for any Christian: We belong to God. No Christian can fall short of that. No person who is such can fail to be holy.[2]

The whole article is well worth reading. It was published at a time when I was coming to the same understanding of holiness, and it helped me clarify my thought on the subject.

As we proceed with our study, we shall see more and more how valuable this understanding of holiness can be.

Chapter 4:
All Have Sinned

All have sinned and fall short of the glory of God (Rom. 3:23).

Anyone with a little understanding of right and wrong can readily see that this is a sinful, wicked world. All one needs to do is to read a newspaper, watch TV news, or just get out and look around. This is especially obvious to us who live in a metropolitan area. The evening news just now began with stories of several murders and continued with several other vicious crimes. There is time in thirty minutes for them to tell only a few of the worst crimes committed. A multitude of other crimes are committed every day that do not even get in the local newspapers.

Thinking about the world in this way can easily lead us to think pessimistically that the whole world is completely under the control of the devil and that there is no one in the world who can be trusted. But it is not really true that everyone is a criminal. There are probably millions in this city who have not committed any murders, burglaries, or other such serious crimes and never will. Many of them are good, moral people who would not consider breaking such laws. They might sometimes drive a little over the speed limit, or jaywalk if they thought it was safe. But they are not criminals. They are good neighbors and help one another in a variety of ways.

What about the good moral people of the world? Are they good in the sight of God? How could God call such people sinners?

Sin Is a Theological Word

The fact is that the word *sin* is not a legal term but rather theological. It does not mean breaking the laws of the land, but much more than that. Sin has to do, not with our relationship with the courts of the land, but with God. It is not merely doing what could cause one to be put in jail, but doing what would break fellowship with God, our Creator. It is for this reason that Paul could say that "all have sinned."

Now if we look at the context of this passage in Romans 3, we see that Paul was writing to the church in Rome, which he had never visited, but which he was hoping to preach in soon. He was making here his most systematic presentation of the gospel message which he had preached elsewhere, and which he was planning to preach in Rome.

Paul's way of expounding the gospel to the Romans was to begin by explaining that all needed the gospel in the same way. He showed first that all the Gentiles had sinned and therefore needed the gospel. Then he showed that all the Jews had sinned and that they needed salvation in Christ just as did the Gentiles. No one in the whole world could stand up before God and self-righteously declare that he or she did not need salvation. "For no human being will be justified in his sight by works of the law, since through the law comes knowledge of sin" (Rom. 3:20).

All Scripture agrees with this assessment of the human condition. If we look to the Old Testament, we see a host of statements that support the fact. "There is no man who does not sin" (1 Kings 8:46). Solomon, in his prayer at the dedication of the Temple, remarked, "There is no man who does not sin" (2 Chron. 6:36). Paul, in Romans 3:10-18, quotes six other passages from the Old Testament to show that all have sinned.

Look also at some other passages of the New Testament that make the same declaration.

And you he made alive, when you were dead through the trespasses and sins in which you once walked, following the course of this world, following the prince of the power of the air, the spirit that is now at work in the sons of disobedience. (Eph. 2:1-3).

If we say we have not sinned, we make him a liar, and his word is not in us (1 John 1:10).

Human Experience Agrees

A look within your own heart will no doubt cause you to say that you must confirm the biblical statements that all have sinned. Who can say that he or she has never sinned against God? The only person who is not aware of past sin is the one who does not have an adequate conception of the holiness and glory of God.

The fact is that as soon as people understand enough about God to comprehend something of the meaning of sin, they recognize that sin is universal. The idea that all have sinned is so widely accepted that all too many think that there is no way to escape from sin. They come to feel that sin is an inescapable part of being human. If asked if they sin, they reply, "Of course. I'm human!"

This universal experience of sin, however, makes problems because of the way some think. It is too easy to feel that if everyone sins, then sin is not so bad after all. Since there is no one who has not sinned, whenever we sin, we can feel that we have plenty of company. Thus the very concept of the universality of sin can be used by many as a means of escaping the feeling of guilt. It is a way to exonerate one's self. It is common for a sinner to enjoy seeing the sins of others, since it makes them feel less sinful. This is why it is so necessary to hold up the holiness of God before all. Only a vision of the holiness of God can show a sinner his own sin. This is why the convicting work of the Holy Spirit is so necessary (John 15:8-11).

Sin Is Against God

One of the things that helps us to see the seriousness of sin in spite of seeing its universality, is to see that sin is always sin against God. David saw this very clearly when he came to recognize how terribly he had sinned. He prayed to God:

Against thee, thee only, have I sinned, and done that which is evil in thy sight, so that thou art justified in thy sentence and blameless in thy judgment (Ps. 51:4).

Now the fact is that David had sinned grievously against Bathsheba, against her relatives and friends, against her husband, against his court which trusted him, and against the nation as a whole. All this he knew full well. But he also knew the seriousness of sinning against God, and knew that this was the most important aspect of his sinning. He knew that nothing else could be set right about the whole mess unless he could get right with God first.

The fact that sin is always against God emphasizes the awful sinfulness of sin. It is far worse than simply hurting one of our friends, or even ourselves. Sin is never a private matter but always affects God, and in one way or another it affects others. This means that no one has the right to live a sinful life, thinking that it is his or her own personal choice to which he or she has an inalienable right. One who makes such a choice is choosing to go against the will and purpose of God and is thus alienating himself or herself from God and his blessing. This is exactly what each of us has done. For all have sinned.

Results of Sin

Sin makes one a slave. Jesus said, "Truly, truly, I say to you, every one who commits sin is a slave to sin" (John 8:34). And this fact is confirmed by all, for everyone who has not been made free from sin is enslaved by it. Of course, this is more obvious as we look at certain sins involving drugs, or gambling, or the like. We are all familiar with the person who is enslaved to some such kind of vice. We feel pity for such a one and for those who are hurt by such slavery of a friend or relative. But we must not let this blind us to the fact that every sin is enslaving. No matter what one does against God, the very act of rebelling against God makes one a slave to sin.

Paul treats of the slavery of sin in Romans 6:12-20. He here contrasts the slavery to sin with the voluntary love-service to God that is characteristic of the Christian. He declares that we must understand that "if you yield yourselves to any one as obedient slaves, you are slaves of the one whom you obey, either of sin, which leads to death, or of obedience, which leads to righteousness" (v. 16).

Since every human being seems to have a strong desire to be free and to feel free, this slavery to sin brings misery to the sinner. To avoid this misery people may try to fill life with busyness. But at times one feels the bondage of sin and longs to be free.

Likewise, one never feels his or her bondage to sin so much as when one begins to try to return to God. And the harder one seeks to break away from sin and be reconciled to God, the more the bondage to sin chafes. Part of the work of the Holy Spirit causes the person to feel the bondage of sin enough to give it up and plead for mercy from God. As Jesus said, "He will convince the world concerning sin and righteousness and judgment" (John 16:8).

Sin Blinds to Goodness

In addition to the binding power of sin is its blinding power. The longer one goes on in sin, the more blind one is to the goodness of God, the beauty of the world, and the good things that ought to be done. This comes about in much the same way as when a parent calls a child. If the child does not respond the first time or two, that child apparently becomes deaf to the call, and does not even notice. Soon the child can honestly say, "I did not know you called."

One sin causes a certain blindness to the will of God that makes it easier to sin again. Any willful turning away from

35

what one knows to be right makes one more blind to the right. This is dangerous because one becomes less and less aware of how far he or she has drifted. If awareness does come, it may be too late.

Sin Brings Death

When we referred to Ephesians 2:1-3 we saw clearly that the sinner is dead in his or her sins. This is a spiritual death, which is more frightening than physical death, because this death is eternal—unless through Christ one is resurrected before the coming of physical death. "It is appointed for men to die once, and after that comes judgment" (Heb. 9:27). Jesus stated clearly that when the resurrection day comes, we will all be raised up from the dead, but whether that is good or bad for us will depend on our life in this world. "The hour is coming when all who are in the tombs will hear his voice and come forth, those who have done good, to the resurrection of life, and those who have done evil, to the resurrection of judgment" (John 5:28-29).

Through John, Christ wrote to the church in Sardis: "I know your works; you have the name of being alive, and you are dead" (Rev. 3:1). He did not mean that the whole church was dead, as he explained in verse 4, but that many of them were, because of their sin. What a tragedy it is to be spiritually dead and not even be aware of it! This is what sin does.

The Wrath of God

Sin brings the wrath of God on the sinner. This is repeatedly stated in the Old Testament.

And the LORD'S anger was kindled against Israel, and he made them wander in the wilderness forty years, until all the generation that had done evil in the sight of the LORD was consumed (Num. 32:13).

You shall not go after other gods, of the gods of the peoples who are round about you; for the LORD your God in the midst of you is a jealous God; lest the anger of the LORD your God be kindled against you, and he destroy you from off the face of the earth (Deut. 6:14-15).

A host of similar passages could be quoted from the Old Testament, but it must not be thought that the New Testament is different. We must not cherish the common idea that the wrath of God has no place in the gospel message. In the very same chapter that tells us of the love of God for the world, we read of the wrath of God: "He who believes in the Son has eternal life; he who does not obey the Son shall not see life, but the wrath of God rests upon him" (John 3:36). There are at least twenty-six references in the New Testament to the wrath of God.

While the emphasis in the New Testament is on the grace and mercy of God, clearly this mercy will come to an end, and then will come the Day of Wrath. This wrath of God is not uncontrolled anger, as in human beings, but rather the right and just retribution for the sin of turning away from the love and mercy of God to do one's own will. One can do this if he or she so chooses, but then come the consequences. Mercy will not have the last word. Justice will be done in the end.

The "wrath" of God means something like God's justice. What is meant is that each person will receive from God just what God knows he or she deserves at the final judgment. When Jesus comes again, it will be for final judgment, and the day of God's mercy will be over. This will be the final effect of sin.

All Need Salvation

Since we have seen that all have sinned in the sight of God, it is obvious that all need salvation in Christ Jesus. Paul made this clear:
A man is not justified by works of the law but through faith in Jesus Christ, even we have believed in Christ Jesus, in order to be justified by faith in Christ, and not by works of the law, because by works of the law shall no one be justified (Gal. 2:16).

By the expression "works of the law," Paul is saying that one cannot be justified before God on the basis of never having sinned or broken the Law, for all have sinned. So we must be justified on another basis, and that basis is the mercy of God as revealed in Jesus Christ.

The point established in this chapter is that all have sinned against God and therefore need salvation. This can only be obtained by trusting in the mercy of God, not in our own goodness. What we need to establish next, by the word of God, is that we do not need to go on sinning all our lives, but that we can have victory over sin even in this present world. To do this, we must first look carefully at the meaning of the word *sin* as it is used in the Bible.

Chapter 5:
A Right Concept of Sin

At this point you may be wondering why we need to spend so much time on the subject of sin when our study concerns holiness. This is a good question, but it also has a good answer.

The fact is that the biblical concept of holiness cannot be understood unless one first understands just what sin is, as the Bible speaks of it. It may be surprising to see just how central to theology the concept of sin must be. If we are wrong on this point, we are apt to be wrong in our whole theology.

Consider, for example, the fact that Jesus died for our sins, and to save us from sin (Matt. 1:21). If we have a false concept of what sin is, we will have a false idea of why Christ died, and of what he really came to do. And since Christ and his life and work are the heart of the gospel, one is basically wrong in his or her understanding of the gospel because of a wrong concept of sin.

Richard S. Taylor wrote a book on this subject in which he had some very important points to make on the relationship between the concept of sin and the rest of theology:

> Sin, as one doctrine of the Christian system, is the common denominator of the other doctrines. . . . Since the question of sin is so basically related to the nature of

God and the plan of redemption, it is the one doctrine by which all others can be reduced to their simplest significance. Furthermore, it forms the surest and most logical measuring stick by which the accuracy of those doctrines can be detected.

> The doctrines relating to sin form the center around which we build our entire theological system.[1]

By the last statement, he did not mean that sin is the center of his own theology only, but of every theology. The concept of sin is the starting point of theology, since sin is what is wrong with the human race and is what keeps us from God and his fellowship. No sure cure for the ills of the human race can be found unless we know just what the malady is. This is true with our physical ills as well.

I was once treated by a very good doctor for the wrong illness. He treated me for polio for some time until he found that I did not have polio at all, but a very different disease which can cause some of the same preliminary symptoms. I did not begin to get better until the correct diagnosis was made. In the same way, if we are mistaken about the true nature of sin, which causes all people to need salvation, then we will also be mistaken about the remedy for sin, which is the gospel of Jesus Christ, and we will be mistaken about holiness, which is the result of accepting God's remedy. So we must pay close attention to the meaning of sin if we are to understand holiness.

Probably the best way to clarify this matter is to look at some nonbiblical concepts and see how they affect other aspects of theology.

Nonbiblical Concepts

1. *Sin is ignorance.* Many thinkers of all ages have thought that the only trouble with human beings is that they do not know enough about right and wrong, or that they do not know how to do the right. Socrates seemed to express this view at times in ancient Greece, and others in ages since have done the same. The idea was common in the old liberal

theology of the early part of the twentieth century.

Now this concept of sin gives the impression of being very optimistic. If all that is wrong with people is ignorance, then all we need to do is to educate them. Education can solve all the ills of the world. Education would empty the prisons and make crime obsolete. But the problem is seen to be much more complicated and deeper than that, when we see that some of the worst criminals are highly educated.

One clear example of the fallacy of this idea is seen in the sexual crimes and sins of our age. For decades we have been told that the reason for the increase of unwed parents multiplying and getting younger and younger is ignorance. The proper sex education will solve all the problems, we are told. And we can see that there is some truth in this. But if this were the whole truth, or even the most important aspect of the truth, we can see that doctors and nurses would never commit sexual sins. This is not the case.

It is all too common for people to sin, not because they do not know any better, but because they are enticed by their natural desires and express or fulfill those desires in sinful ways. The very best education is no guarantee that one will not sin.

Notice, then, what effect this idea has on the rest of one's theology. If one believes that sin is caused by ignorance, that person will not believe in missions or evangelism, but only in education. One will not seek to provide churches, but schools. One will not seek to evangelize and persuade persons to believe in Christ but will wait for education to make the person better. This is the reason some church leaders in the world have made the suggestion that we stop all mission work, at least for a while. The whole gospel of Christ is watered down by this false concept of sin.

2. *Sin as evolutionary lag.* In the last century a growing feeling on the part of some was that sins are merely left-over forms of behavior that were appropriate in some former stage of development, but that in later stages are no longer appropriate or right. For example, at one time fighting for territorial rights as do lions or monkeys may have been the

41

proper way of establishing ownership. But now in this more enlightened and highly organized society, it is wrong to act like animals. One should instead use the law courts and legal methods to accomplish the same purpose.

Some non-Christian anthropologists and comparative psychologists keep suggesting that most, if not all, of our anti-social and criminal behavior is caused by innate modes of behavior; these behaviors were good at an earlier stage of evolution, whether a human stage, or prehuman, but they are now considered wrong. We frequently see such articles in books, newspapers, and magazines. Sin, then, is not a serious matter, but just something left over from an earlier stage. We will soon outgrow it, or evolve beyond it.

Futurists make much of this concept. They tell us of future ages that will no longer have war, crimes, criminals, or prisons. This grows naturally out of the concept of sin. If this is true, then sin is not to be too deeply deplored. The cure is not salvation in Christ, but only the natural process of evolution, which will make it obsolete, sometime.

3. *Sin as finiteness.* Both Paul Tillich and Reinhold Niebuhr have held that sin grows naturally out of a person's understanding that he or she is infinite. So the real problem with the human race is that human beings were created. They are lower than God, and they hate it. They refuse to worship God because they would rather *be* god.

Niebuhr did not say that being finite is sin but that it is the root and source of sin. So the basic sin is wanting to break out of finitude and be a god. Certain psychologists have also advocated a concept similar to this, blaming all the sin of humankind on human limitation. Human beings want to be free, but they find that their freedom is severely limited. It is only relative freedom. All sin results from the anxiety caused by the frustrated desire for infinite freedom.

In a very real sense, this concept of sin may have some value or truth in it. A human being is finite. Human freedom is severely limited. Human beings commonly seek to rise above this limitation and be their own boss. But if that is all there is to sin, then God is to be blamed for making us like this. God made us finite creatures, and if this concept is correct, it means that God put us in a situation in which sin is unavoidable. It is not really our fault, but God's. How could we then be guilty, if sin is the result of God's creating us?

4. *Sin as inherent in the physical.* Plato considered sin to be an inevitable part of the physical. Only spirit was good, he thought. So the good spirit is imprisoned in the evil physical body and is doomed to be evil until the soul or spirit escapes from the prison of the physical.

This anthropological dualism of spirit and flesh was basic to Greek thought and has been adopted into much Christian thinking. But it is basically contrary to biblical thought, as we shall see more clearly later. It leads to false conclusions about much of our theology and has caused untold confusion about holiness. So we shall have to give considerable attention to the idea. But for the present, it is sufficient for us to see what it does in general terms.

A little thought makes it obvious that if sin is a basic and inherent part of the physical body, then holiness is impossible for any human being, at least while still alive. For the only way goodness is possible is for the soul to be freed from the body, since the body is evil. The only way to be holy, then, is to die. At death the soul is separated from the body, and holiness is not only possible, but natural. One who believes in this way thinks of the holy soul as imprisoned in a sinful body. It is then no longer the soul that sins, but the body.

This ancient Greek concept has not usually been so baldly stated by Christian thinkers. Yet a tendency toward it can be detected in some Christians. Wherever it is found, it causes the whole theology to go wrong. This may be one of the reasons why so many feel that holiness is impossible, whether the reasoning is ever expressed in words or not. The feeling is common that a human being cannot possibly ever please God because God is so perfect and infinitely good. But this would mean that God had made us in such a way that we could never hope to please him in this life. We would have to wait until after death.

The fact is that some theologians say that entire sanctification in this life is impossible; we must wait until death for holiness to be conferred on us. It is built on the implication that being a human being is inherently sinful. If that is true then it must be because God made us sinful. Further, it would make death the sanctifying power, rather than the Holy Spirit. It would mean that God is not able to save us from all sin in this present life. So it distorts the gospel from beginning to end. Now that we have seen something of the major nonbiblical concepts of sin, and of what they do to theology, it is time for us to look at what the Bible says about sin. We will begin by examining some of the Hebrew and Greek words for sin and see something of the way they are used in the Bible.

Biblical Words for Sin

1. *Missing the Mark.* The first time the word "sin" occurs in the English Bible is in Genesis 4:7, when God was speaking to Cain. The Hebrew word used here is *chattath*. The Septuagint, the pre-Christian Greek translation of the Hebrew Old Testament, uses here the word *hamartano*. These are the most common biblical words for sin and both have the same root meaning, "to miss the mark."

We must be careful not to draw wrong conclusions from the root meaning of these two words. Since they mean "missing the mark," sin is often said to be blamed on poor aim. We try to live for God, but, being human, we miss the mark we aim at. This is simply not true. This interpretation makes sin to be not a willful turning from God and his way, but simply a natural human failure of achievement. Nothing could be much further from the biblical concept of sin.

Note, for example, the way the word is used here in the story of Cain. What was the sin of Cain? Was it that he tried his best to do the right thing but failed? Not at all. God warned him that he could do right if he chose, but that if he chose to go on in his wrong attitude, he would commit a sin.

The Lord said to Cain, "Why are you angry, and why

44

has your countenance fallen? If you do well, will you not be accepted? And if you do not do well sin is couching at the door; its desire is for you, but you must master it" (Gen. 4:6-7).

Clearly God was telling Cain that he was on dangerous ground morally. Yet Cain could conquer sin if he so chose! "You must master it," God said. God would not keep him from sinning if he chose to do so, but God plainly told Cain that he could and must keep himself from sin. So the word *chattath* does not mean poor aim, but rather, wrong will, and wrong choice. This is consistent with the teaching of the rest of the Bible in the use of both *chattath* and *harartano*. To sin is to will to do wrong. Sin is a willful transgression of the law and will of God.

We see the same thing in Genesis 18:20 when God said, "The outcry against Sodom and Gomorrah is great and their sin is very grave." Here again the Hebrew word is used, but it is obviously not used with its root meaning of failing to hit the mark aimed at, but rather it refers to sin that is willfully and maliciously committed. The sin was so great that God destroyed the two cities.

When David had sinned with Bathsheba and had arranged for her husband to be killed and subsequently had come to see his guilt, he said to Nathan the prophet, "I have sinned against the Lord" (2 Sam. 12:13). Here the verb form of the same Hebrew word is used *(chatta')*. But his sin was far more than a careless blunder or ignorant mistake. It is not that he tried to do right but failed because of his human lack of ability to do better.

He was tempted, and then instead of turning from temptation, he deliberately decided to yield to temptation and sinned grievously. One sin led to another. Adultery led to murder, which he hoped would never be discovered. This sin was not a failure of ability, but a deliberate sin against God. And David knew it was true.

When Isaiah was writing a scathing denunciation of the wickedness, stubbornness, and lawlessness of the people who were supposed to be the people of God, he called them a sinful (*chatte'*) nation (Isa. 1:4). He used this same word that we have been discussing. And in Isaiah 59:2, he pointed out to them that "your sins have hid his face from you." Sin is a deliberate turning away from God and causes separation from God.

When we turn to the New Testament, the corresponding Greek word for sin is *hamartia* (noun) and *hamartano* (verb). This word has the same etymological history as *chatta'* and the same so-called root meaning. It is also used in exactly the same way as the Hebrew word, with the same meaning. To say that it means "missing the mark" is to miss the mark. It is not used to mean poor aim, but aiming at something other than the will of God. This fact is spelled out most explicitly in 1 John 3:4 in which we find the statement, "*He hamartia estin he anomia*" ("Sin is lawlessness"). *Anomia* means "lawlessness, anarchy, the refusal to do what one knows that he ought to do." So John is insisting that sin is a deliberate, willful choice of wrong rather than right. This is an important point and settles the meaning of the word so far as biblical usage is concerned.

We have spent considerable time on these two Hebrew and Greek words because they are the generic terms for sin in the Bible, and because their meaning is so often distorted. It has all too often been asserted that sin is merely "missing the mark" through unavoidable human failure to do better. If God made human beings in such a way that they could not help but sin, then how could a just God ever condemn human beings from sinning? Where could justice be found in that?

A careful study of the uses of these two words in the Old Testament shows that they are consistently used to mean willful doing of wrong, not merely unavoidable human failure of aim. It is not that human beings try their best but fail because it is impossible to succeed. Sin is the deliberate turning away from what one knows to be right or the will of God. It is true that Leviticus 4:13-14 refers to an offering for sins ignorantly committed. But obviously no one could offer such a sacrifice until the person did know that what he or she had done was a sin. When the person was no longer ignorant and knew that he or she had sinned, the sacrifice was offered. Sin was only true sin when the person came to know that what he or she had done was wrong. Then a person becames guilty of sin. Then a person stubbornly refusing to right a wrong would not be forgiven. Sin is the result of knowingly, willfully doing wrong.

2. *Sin as crookedness.* The Old Testament uses the word *avon*, which suggests crookedness or perversion. It means crooked in the sense of not being straight. It is used 231 times and is sometimes translated *iniquity, guilt,* or *punishment.*

3. *Sin as rebellion. Pasha'* is the Hebrew word for rebellion, revolt, or refusal to do God's will. It could be used of civil rebellion, such as when Israel rebelled against the rule of David (1 Kings 12:19). But it is more often used for the rebellion against God.

Pasha' is used eighty-six times in the Old Testament and certainly expresses the most profound theological meaning of the word *sin.* Sin is basically rebellion against the rule of God. Sin is a person rebelling against the personal creator and ruler of all. So sin is a slap in the face to God, an affront that cannot go unpunished. This fact is well expressed by Kohler:

> Essentially and in the last resort in the Old Testament revelation, sin is not the violation of objective command-ments and prohibitions and not the iniquities which demonstrate their weakness and folly (1 Chron. 21:8) and perversity. *Sin is revolt of the human will against the divine will.*[2]

4. *Sin as wickedness. Rasha'* is the Old Testament word usually translated as *wickedness.* The wicked person is volun-tarily turning himself or herself against God and his will and is personally responsible for his or her wickedness. This is seen clearly in Ezekiel's statement, "When the wicked man turns away from the wickedness he has committed and does what is lawful and right, he shall save his life" (Ezek. 18:27).

47

The sinner turned from God and he or she must turn back to God.

5. *Sin as unfaithfulness.* Sin is often called *ma'al*, meaning "unfaithfulness." This is especially important when we remember that the people of God were bound to him by a covenant. To turn from God was to be unfaithful to the covenant promise they had made. It was like unfaithfulness to a spouse, and this is often said, especially in the prophets.

6. *Sin as evil. Ra'* is the word that means evil in contrast to the good. It can be used of bad fruit (Jer. 24:2), of bad actions, or bad events. The corresponding Greek words are *poneros* and *phaulos*, which are used of sin and of more general badness.

7. *Sin as iniquity.* The Hebrew word is *avel* which is often translated *iniquity*. However, it is difficult to make a consistent distinction between the significance of this word and some of the others, such as *chatta'* or *rasha'*. So this word is often rendered by such words as *wicked, unrighteous,* and *perverse.*

8. *Sin as unrighteousness.* Besides the New Testament words we have already considered, we find the Greek word *adikia*, which means unrighteousness, wrongdoing, or injustice. It means what is wrong in the sight of God. It is what keeps us from God. It keeps God from approving us and our lives.

9. *Sin as unfaithfulness.* The Greek word *apistia* corresponds with the Hebrew *ma'al*, with its meaning of unfaithfulness or unbelief. But the idea of unfaithfulness is most basic to its use in the Bible. It stresses not just the lack of belief or faith but rather rebellion or turning away from God.

10. *Sin as transgression. Paraptoma* and *parabasis* both mean walking in some way other than the right way. They do not refer primarily to falling or stumbling out of the way, but to deliberate turning aside from the right.

11. *Sin as debauchery.* The Greek *aselgia* means unbridled lust or shamelessness. Paul contrasts the Christian with wicked persons of the world who has given themselves over to debauchery (*aselgia*). Christians control themselves and are controlled by their love for Christ and do not give

48

themselves over to sensual pleasures in that way.

12. *Sin as perverted desire.* Desire in itself is not evil, but any desire can be perverted into something evil. This is expressed by the Greek *epithumia*, meaning perverted desire. Desire for food is not evil, but it can be perverted into an all-consuming gluttony, which is not only evil in itself, but can lead to further sins. The desire to be comfortable is good, but when perverted it keeps one from being and doing what one should.

But desire must not be limited to the sensuous. It includes the all-too common desire to assert oneself against God and his will. This desire to be one's own boss is behind the rebellion that is the essence of sin. We see it first of all in the desire of Adam and Eve to assert their own will against that of God, and to decide for themselves what they would or would not do. This was their sin. And it is repeated in the life of every person.

13. *Sin as irreverence.* The Greek word *asebeia* is most naturally translated *irreverence.* But sometimes it is rendered *ungodliness.* It means something like irreligious, or godless. The person acts as though God does not exist.

14. *Sin as evil.* This is indicated by words such as *poneros, kakia,* and *phaulos.* As we have indicated before, these words point to what is wrong, as over against the right. But this evil is a terrible thing, because it has been so utterly opposed to God.

15. *Sin as hostility.* Greek *echthra* is the word that speaks of the sinner's hostility to God and is often rendered *enmity.* The sinner is the enemy of God. Sin is the personal hatred toward God that causes the sinner to rebel against him and his rule. James pointed out that "friendship with the world is enmity *(echthra)* with God" (James 4:4). And Paul says, "For the mind that is set on the flesh is hostile [*echthra*] to God; it does not submit to God's law, indeed it cannot; and those who are in the flesh cannot please God" (Rom. 8:7-8).

So many false concepts of sin have been built on the interpretation of the words for sin in the Bible that the words must be considered in their context, not apart from the

49

context. It is not the history of a word, or it's root meaning, that tells us what it means, but rather the use that is made of the word in particular contexts. This point, which has not been understood by some of the excellent Bible scholars of the last century, has been made very clear by the work of such writers as James Barr and Moises Silva. While recognizing that we cannot agree with either of these writers in overall theology, we can learn much from them and accept their wisdom gladly. James Barr puts his major thesis in these words:

> Theological thought of the type found in the New Testament has its characteristic linguistic expression not in the word individually but in the word-combination or sentence. . . . The attempt to relate the individual word directly to the theological thought leads to the distortion of the semantic contribution made by words in contexts; the value of the context comes to be seen as something contributed by the word, and then it is read into the word as its contribution where the context is in fact different.[3]

Barr's point is that we cannot learn what a word means in a particular context and then use that particular meaning to be sure what it means in every other place. The context can affect the meaning of a word. A second major point Barr makes in his whole work is that etymology—the history of the development of a word—is not a clear and decisive indication of its meaning at any particular time. Silva makes the point more clear with an illustration apropos to our study:

> The point is that we learn much more about the doctrine of sin by John's statement, "Sin is the transgression of the law," than by a wordstudy of hamartia; similarly, tracing the history of the word hagios is relatively unimportant for the doctrine of sanctification once we have examined Romans 6-8 and related passages.[4]

This is so important, and so little understood by Bible

readers and preachers, that we must be sure no one got lost in the fog of this discussion. To review one point, the word *hamartia* is usually said to mean "to miss the mark, to fail to achieve a goal." This is based on the so-called root-meaning of the Greek word, or on its etymology or supposed etymology. The fact is that we do not know as much as we wish we did about the etymology of Greek and Hebrew words, and much of what is given in the lexicons is speculation. But even if we were sure of the original meaning of this word, we can be sure that that is not the way it is used in the Bible. The root meaning of a word is not usually its present meaning. The root meaning of *pen* is *feather*, but knowing this would not help anyone recognize a pen when he or she saw one for the first time. The root meaning of *magazine* is "granary, warehouse." But that does not add much to our understanding of *Vital Christianity.*

The Biblical Concept of Sin

We might begin with a negative consideration of the erroneous concepts of sin. Without listing and refuting each of them at this point, we can say that the basic error of false views of sin is that they minimize the sinner's responsibility and guilt for his or her own sin. The sinner has sinned and is only too glad to blame the sin on someone or something else. She longs to show that she could not help committing a sin. Or he grasps at any straw that will put at least some of the blame elsewhere.

For example, too much emphasis on the etymological meaning of *hamartia* as "missing the mark" has led some to explain it as mere human failure to do what one tries to do. But the fact is that *sin is not poor aim, but a deliberate aiming in the wrong direction.* Explaining the word *paraptoma* as meaning "falling by the way" to show that sin is mere stumbling through human frailty, has led to a similar result.

An even worse error is seen in the definition of sin as "any falling short of the glory and perfection of God." Such a definition is standard with some groups of Christians, but it leads to a total misunderstanding of sin, salvation, and

51

holiness. It means that sin is totally unavoidable for human beings so long as we are in this body and in this world. God made us less than himself, and if it is sin to be less than God is, then we are by creation sinful. There is no escape from this conclusion. And all human beings can do in this case is to admit their sin, regret it if they so choose, but recognize that that is the way God made us. In a very real and terrible sense, this is putting the blame for sin on God himself. It cannot be our fault if this is the way it is.

Basic Characteristics

Let us now consider some of the basic characteristics of the biblical concept of sin. Some of them we have at least hinted at or discussed before.

1. *Sin is a theological concept.* Basically, sin is in relation to God and cannot be understood rightly if thought of as separate from God. That is, sin is rebellion against God or turning away from God. Sin may or may not be illegal. It may not be a breaking of civil or criminal law at all. It may not even be an action. But it is refusing or neglecting to love God wholeheartedly, and to serve him unstintingly.

Sin, then, is more than simple failure. It is more than "being human." It cannot be excused on the basis that it is only what is a natural and inevitable part of being human. It is *against God.* I know of no better statement of this important fact than one by Aulen:

> It cannot be sufficiently emphasized that sin is a concept which belongs entirely to the religious realm. As soon as we remove it from this sphere, it loses its essential significance. We do not speak of sin in a juridical environment or in criminal justice. There it is simply a case of crime and transgression of law. To inject the concept of sin in this connection would be to inject an irrelevant category. In the same way a non-religious philosophy of morals and ethics cannot use the word sin . . . On the contrary, faith cannot avoid speaking about sin. . . . Sin is a concept that is inseparably con-

nected with the relationship to God. There is no sin which is not sin against God. It is meaningless to talk about sin if it is no relation to God (Ps. 51:4). . . . From the viewpoint of Christian faith it would be meaningless to divide sin into two classes: sins against God and sins against the neighbor . . . To say that the concept of sin belongs entirely in the religious sphere is the same as saying that all sin is sin against God.[5]

2. *Sin is freely chosen.* Sin is not something that simply happens to persons against their will but is chosen by the individual in freedom, and that individual is responsible for his or her choice. The sinner did not necessarily think about the act or the attitude a long time, weighing all the consequences and pros and cons, and then made a choice. The person may or may not have done so. But sin is from the heart—the will. Sin is not some *thing* inside people that causes them to do as they do, but rather sin is the whole person oriented in the wrong direction. This is what is meant by saying that sin is from the will or heart of the person. The individual sinner is responsible for his or her own sin. The Bible never separates sin from freedom and responsibility. Yet many definitions of sin do just that.

If we think of sin as any falling short of the perfection of God, then of course all of us are sinful and we must remain so as long as we live. None of us can hope to reach the perfection of God's knowledge, wisdom, and justice. We are not God and cannot match his infinite love, understanding, or any other divine perfection. This would mean that all of us sin every day. And this is what is meant by many who oppose the concept of holiness. They keep insisting that none of us match the perfection of God. But that of course is not what is meant by the term sin in the Bible. For example, John did not say that sin is any lack of perfect obedience to all the laws of God. What he said was that sin is lawlessness. The Greek word *anomia* means opposition to law, willful disobedience to law, lawlessness. It is much more than a simple failure, through lack of understanding or ability, to obey the Law perfectly. It is turning away from God's will to do one's own will.

Sin, then, is not mistakes of ignorance or blunders through inability to do what God requires, but it is refusal to be bound by God's will. God does not hold a person accountable for what he or she is incapable of doing. As a parent, God does not condemn the individual for the lack of ability to do all what God wants him or her to do eventually. God knows very well what we can and cannot do, and he does not condemn us for what we cannot help.

At first glance some may think that to make sin any falling short of the perfection of God would be to exalt God. Some may assumed that this requirement of absolute perfection is a deeper concept of sin. But such is not the case. To say this is the nature of sin is to say that we are all sinful and cannot help it and cannot ever hope to be anything else. It is to say that God made us human and he condemns us for not being God. Further, it gives every sinner an excuse for his or her sin, so that one can say, "Yes, I sin all the time. That proves I am human. I am just like everyone else. So this definition of sin, while it may seem better at first glance, leads to the destruction of the feeling of guilt. It leads to the concept of sin as normal for human beings.

God assures us through the whole Bible that we are definitely responsible for sin. Sin is what we *will* to do. So sin is our own choice, made in freedom and for which we are responsible.

3. *Sin is personal.* Any definition of sin that tends to make sin impersonal is false, because it minimizes guilt. If we think of sin as something within the person that controls the person or causes one to do wrong, then sin is impersonal. If sin is something within me, then I am not really responsible for it. This is the way it minimizes guilt.

It is vital for us to remember that sin is not something impersonal, but has to do with our personal relationship with God. It is personal because we are persons and because God is a Person. When theologians say that God is a Person, they do not at all mean that God is human, but that he is not *impersonal*. God is all that is involved in being a person, with mind, will, consciousness, and infinitely more. Except for the physical body, God has all the intellectual, moral, and spiritual qualities of a human being, but in infinite perfection.

One of the basic errors of our thought about God is to think of him, or treat him as though he were a machine. People all too often pray to God as though he were a prayer-answering machine. If we just put in enough prayers of the right kind and quantity, we will surely get just what we want! But this is not true. God is personal. Prayer is a two-way conversation. God seldom, if ever, answers us in audible words, but God's Spirit wants to help us to grow in the way we pray and in the kinds of things for which we pray. God is not in the business of growing dependent babies but mature Christians. So God does not give us everything we ask for, but he wants us to learn to ask for more important things— more important to him; not necessarily to us. This is one aspect of what we mean by saying God is personal.

Now consider what this personal aspect of God does for our concept of sin.

Since we are persons, and God is personal, sin is rebellion against God. Sin is turning away from God. Sins are those actions, attitudes, and dispositions that result from being turned away from God. We must not try to define sin, then, in any impersonal way.

A. H. Strong defines sin as "lack of conformity to the moral law of God, whether in act, disposition, or state."[6] This is practically the same as that in the Westminster Shorter Catechism. This is good, as far as it goes, but the word *law* is misleading because it sounds too impersonal. A better expression would be something like "the known will of God" or "God's will for a person." We would do even better if we would note that sin is the opposite of the love for God that we ought to have.

No definition of sin can be scriptural if it does not include personal responsibility. That is why Wesley's famous definition is that "sin is the willful transgression of the known will of God." Likewise, it is why Harris and Taylor define sin as "accountable wrongness before God."[7]

A Definition

After all this we can suggest that sin can be defined as "turning away from God and sins are those actions, attitudes, or dispositions that follow from being turned away from God."

Sin, then, is neither some part of a person, nor something inside of a person. Sin is the whole person oriented in the wrong direction. However, when we define sin thus, we must remember that we are making a distinction between sin—which brings about the separation of the soul from God—and sins, which are the actions, attitudes, and dispositions that result from that separation.

"Sin is the voluntary separation of the human will from God."[8] This is Pope's helpful way of putting it. Such expression is near to the heart of what the whole Bible teaches about sin. We often say that sin separates us from God, but to speak more accurately the voluntary turning away from God is what sin is. It is not something done to a person, since the person is the one who does the separating. The turning away from God is what we mean by sin. Sin is the result of turning away from God. Once a person has sinned, that person will commit many sins, because that person is no longer living in the love and fear of God.

Chapter 6:
Original Sin

All have sinned and fall short of the glory of God (Rom. 3:23).

The Bible teaches the universality of sin. The biblical teaching that all have sinned is clear, abundant, and explicit. But the Bible does not say why all have sinned. The Bible simply does not explain what causes every person who has come to sufficiently mature to make a responsible moral decision, to turn to sin. The Bible says it does happen but does not tell us why.

Yet we like to know why. So, like little children who have first learned the word, we keep asking why. Answers have been given, and they have been supported by quoting scriptures. But these answers have to be read into Scripture, since the Bible does not say why all sin.

As we shall see, those passages that are used to support a theory concerning why everyone sins, do not say why. They simply say that all, without God, are sinful. All, without exception, need redemption by the blood of Jesus Christ. Everyone since Adam has sinned against God and must be redeemed. The only exception is the Savior himself, Jesus Christ.

Original Sin

In order to be sure we are clear on the point made, let us consider the common explanation concerning why all sin. The term *original sin* is commonly used to mean that we are all born with some sort of sinful nature, so that we cannot help sinning. This sinful nature is said to have been inherited in some mysterious way from Adam. Several contradictory explanations have been given concerning how this inheritance takes place, since the Bible does not even say it does take place at all. What it does say is that all sin. This is the common explanation, but it is not found in the Bible. The point is that the question is not asked in the Bible, and is not answered. G. C. Berkouwer was a Calvinist, but in his large monograph on sin, he made some wise observations on the subject. In discussing the question of the origin of sin, he questions the legitimacy of our insisting on knowing the answer.

A remarkable relation exists between seeking for the origin of sin and an exculpation or exoneration of one's own person. Whoever reflects on the origin of sin cannot engage himself in a merely theoretical dispute; rather he is engaged, intimately and personally, in what can only be called the problem of sin's guilt. As soon as he refers to a definite evil or a particular guilt he is no longer concerned about a purely logical or abstract theory. Factors of an entirely different sort come into play, and these influence his question of origin decisively. Any "causal" explanation we propose can only be seen, in the practice of living, as a means of fashioning an "indisputable" excuse. . . . Man's feeble efforts to find the deepest "cause" of his guilt can only succeed in fabricating a self-excuse.[1]

He is saying that the natural tendency of humankind is to seek to put the blame for guilt on someone else or on something else. Adam, when he had sinned, sought to put the blame on God. "This woman you gave me. . . ." It is true that he was saying that she was more guilty than he, but it is also true that he was blaming God for having given the woman to him. And when we seek for the ultimate source of sin, we are looking outside ourselves for somewhere to put the blame for our own sin. We are trying to excuse ourselves.

The attempt to excuse ourselves for our own sin in any way is the attempt to escape our guilt. This is not the way of salvation, but the way of death. We do not need to know where sin comes from or how it comes to us. All we need to know is that we have sinned and that we must bear the guilt for our own sin.

Yet it must be admitted that it is natural for us to seek for the origin of sin, just as we seek to understand the ultimate origin of other things. This does not mean that we must have the answer to the search, since we may have to content ourselves to live our lives without knowing the answer. It is one thing for us to seek to understand and quite another to demand that we understand where sin came from and why it is that we all sin.

We need to be clear concerning what we mean by original sin as *Adamic nature* or *innate depravity*. Adamic nature is a term not found in the Bible but used by theologians to mean the sinful nature inherited from Adam because of his original sin. His first sin was the first sin of the human race, and the concept is that each person born into the human race is born with a sinful nature inherited from him. This is called *depravity*, a term that is not used in the Bible. Depravity is the effect of sin on the personality of the sinner. It is called *innate* to signify that it is born into the infant. Innate means exactly the same as *inborn*.

Original sin is a theological term that is not found in the Bible but has been used in theology with a variety of meanings. It is used by many as though its only possible meaning was the same as *Adamic nature* or *innate depravity*. This is not true, however. We shall see that there is another historic meaning.

Depravity

Depravity is a word, as we have seen, that is not used in the Bible, but which is used by theologians to mean the result of sin in the personality of the sinner. Clearly from our experience and from the teaching of the Bible sin has an effect on the sinner, and it makes him or her more and more sinful. Jesus said that "every one who commits sin is a slave to sin" (John 8:34). The sinner is a slave to sin because of the depravity the sin works in the heart or personality of the sinner.

Not only does the sin affect the sinner, but the sin of Adam had an effect on all the human race, since he was the first man, and we are all descended from him. Wesley spoke of the effect of the original sin of Adam when he was asked about its effect on the human race:

> Do you mean [by original sin] the sin which Adam committed in Paradise? That this is imputed to all men, I allow; yea, that by reason thereof 'the whole creation groaneth and travaileth in pain together until now.' But that any will be damned for this alone, I allow not, till you show me where it is written. Bring me plain proof from Scripture, and I submit; but till then I utterly deny it.[2]

Note his insistence that this "depravity," or "original sin," does not bring condemnation to any infant born since Adam. Wesley explained in another place that original sin cannot be called sin in the proper biblical sense because sin, properly speaking, is a willful transgression of God's will or a willful turning away from the will and way of God.

However, Wesley did insist that, while there was no guilt attached to being born with this innate depravity, even an infant requires the grace and mercy of God if he or she is to be accepted by God. He simply suggested that the grace of God automatically was applied to the infant if that infant died.

A different kind of solution is seen in the suggestion that

the infant is not born sinful but is innocent of sin. However, neither is the infant born holy, since holiness is a positive, personally chosen love for God. Holiness is a consciously chosen relationship of love with God. Adam was made holy, as God intended all human beings to be. But when he sinned, he lost that for all of us. So we are born deprived of that holiness—that personal relationship with God through the indwelling Holy Spirit, who pours the love of God into our hearts (Rom. 5:5). So what we call "innate depravity" is more properly "innate deprivity" or deprivation. As H. Orton Wiley put it, "The generally accepted theory of theologians, both Calvinistic and Arminian, is that of privation—a depravity which is the result of deprivation."[3]

C. E. Brown, in writing on this point, sought to clarify the meaning of what he called "inbred sin."

This question as to whether sin is something, like a cancer, or whether it is nothing, like blindness, being, as it is, the absence of something, has puzzled theologians for ages. Undoubtedly it is easier to understand the doctrine of inbred sin as being a reasonable consequence of Adam's transgression if we think of it as the loss of something—just as blindness is not the addition of something, but the loss of something, i.e., the loss of sight. Inbred sin is the loss of the image of God.[4]

If one objects that the absence of something is not enough to account for sin, Dr. Brown shows further that the absence of calcium in the bones is negative, but it makes the bones have a strong tendency to break. The absence of vision makes one have a tendency to run into things and perhaps to stumble and fall.

To go further, it is no light matter to say that the newborn person is deprived of a loving relationship with the Spirit of God. This means that there is no innate love of God. One has not made a freely chosen covenant with God. There is no commitment to God's word or will. There is no understanding of right or wrong. And there is no decision to do

61

right. This is more than enough to account for the fact that all human beings sin.

Terminology

From all this it follows that the terms *inbred sin* and *innate sin* are misleading, since the newborn infant cannot be guilty of sin in the proper biblical sense. "Innate depravity" could more accurately be called innate deprivation, or, to follow the lead of Purkiser, Taylor, and Taylor, to call it "innate deprivity."[5] *Depravity*, then, can be reserved for the positive results and effects of consciously committed personal sin.

Before we look at what the Bible teaches about the origin of sin, let us see some of the things it does not teach. First of all, the Bible does not teach that we sinned before we were born. Not only is there no specific text saying this, but when the disciples once asked Jesus about whether a man had been born blind because he had sinned or his parents had, Jesus said flatly that neither was the case. If we were born with sins already committed, it would certainly be true that we could not be guilty of having chosen to sin! We could not choose to sin until we were capable of choosing responsibly.

The Bible does not say that we are born guilty of the sins of our ancestors or of Adam, our most ancient ancestor. Yet this is what some have taken the idea of original sin to mean. Augustine seems to have done this in his argument with Pelagius. He said that "in Adam" we all sinned. He based this on a mistranslation of Romans 5:12 in the Latin Vulgate. Even with the mistranslation in the Latin, the grammar and the arrangement of words make this interpretation difficult.

Ezekiel has some strong words to say about the idea that anyone dies because of the sins of others, even their own fathers or ancestors:

> The soul that sins shall die. The son shall not suffer for the iniquity of the father, nor the father suffer for the iniquity of the son; the righteousness of the righteous shall be upon himself, and the wickedness of the wicked shall be upon himself (Ezek. 18:20).

This passage clearly says that a person is not guilty of the sins of his or her ancestors. No person is born guilty of the sin of Adam. If one is guilty of sin, it is because that person has sinned. If we could be born guilty of the sins of others, then we would be dying, not because we had sinned, but because we were born into the human race. Ezekiel declares that this would be unfair and unlike God. God knows who has sinned and who has not and does not blame the one who has not sinned. As Bavinck put it, there is "nothing that offends our reason more than to say that the sin of the first man has made other men guilty, namely those men who are so far removed from this source that they would seem to be incapable of participating within it."[6]

Wesleyan theologians have always consistently refused to consider that infants are born guilty of the sin of Adam. It is not the teaching of the Bible and indeed would be contradictory to the clear Bible doctrine. Richard Taylor put it this way: "Wesleyanism has consistently rejected all forms of realism which affirm the personal participation of infants in Adam's sin"[7] If a person is guilty of sin, it is not because of the sin of Adam, but because that person has sinned.

We have been saying that the Bible does not teach that we are born sinning, that we are born guilty of Adam's sin, or that we sinned before we were born. We need to look at the biblical evidence before going further. Many passages are used to support one or another of these ideas, but the basic passage is Romans 5:12-21. Without this passage, it is safe to say that there would be no such concept. The strongest Old Testament passage is Psalm 51:4-5. Let us consider these two passages in detail.

Psalm 51:4-5

Although it cannot be proved, this psalm is usually taken to have been written by David after he had sinned against Bathsheba, and after Nathan the prophet had caused him to feel the heinousness of his sin, so that he was ready to repent. We will assume that this is the true background of the psalm. It is, then, David's prayer for forgiveness. Even if this were not true, the interpretation would not be different, for it must have been written in circumstances quite similar to this.

Against thee, thee only, have I sinned, and done that which is evil in thy sight, So that thou art justified in thy sentence and blameless in thy judgment. Behold, I was brought forth in iniquity, and in sin did my mother conceive me.

How do we interpret a passage like this? Is it meant to be taken literally? Or is it, like much of the poetic literature of the Bible, to be interpreted as poetry? Is this a careful doctrinal statement, like Paul's letters? Or is it the prayer of a man grieving over his own sin? David began this psalm by crying out for the mercy of God upon him because of his sin. His own sin was all he could think of at the moment. He was under the conviction of the Holy Spirit and knew that he wanted forgiveness—the forgiveness of God—more than he wanted anything else in the world.

"Against thee, thee only, have I sinned." Is this really true of David when he had sinned with Bathsheba? We know for sure that it is not the literal truth, for he had sinned against himself. He had sinned against Bathsheba and her husband, Uriah, the Hittite. He had sinned against her family, all his court, and the nation as a whole. But does this mean that this statement in the Bible is not true? Not at all. The word *only* signifies here, as it often does, "primarily."

The first thought anyone ought to have when tempted to do evil is that the sin would be a sin against God. Every sin is a sin against God. It is also a sin against the sinner and a sin against others, but it is first and most of all a sin against God. When Joseph was tempted by the wife of Potiphar, his first thought was "How then can I do this great wickedness, and sin against God?" (Gen. 39:9). In the same way, David knew that he had sinned greatly against himself and the whole nation; but he knew that the most important consideration was that he had sinned against God!

What have we done here with this statement? We have not taken it as a careful doctrinal statement. Nor have we taken it to be false. We have interpreted it as a poetic statement of a heart full of grief for sin. The use of hyperbole to emphasize the basic concept that sin is against God. What was said in this manner truly emphasized the most important and serious aspect of sin. It is just what we need to know.

"Behold, I was brought forth in iniquity, and in sin did my mother conceive me" (v. 5). Here again we need to ask some of the same questions. Is David teaching us that we are born in sin? Is he informing us that he was a sinner before he was born? Is he teaching us that in conceiving him his mother committed sin? Is he saying that marriage is a sin? Clearly the rest of the Bible does not support such ideas. God invented sex and marriage and said that they are good. Sex is right within marriage (Heb. 13:4), so it is not true that his mother sinned in conceiving David. Yet that is the literal meaning of the words of this passage. And the literal meaning of the first part of verse 5 is either that David was born sinful, or that he was born sinning, or that he was born into a sinful world. The last statement is true. But if David was seeking to say that he was sinful when he was born, he could have said so much more clearly and explicitly. If he meant that he was sinning when he was born, he was not using the word *sin* in its usual biblical sense. An infant cannot commit willful sin against God, as the infant is not capable of responsible choice.

How, then, can we interpret this verse? What is it that David was saying? Oesterly comments on this verse:

These words have often been taken to imply the doctrine of original sin; that is a mistake. Judaism has never taught this; the idea that Adam's sin in any way affected the status of the human race is quite alien to Jewish teaching.[8]

David was not putting the blame for his own sin on his mother for conceiving him in sin. Neither was he putting the blame on God for letting him be born sinful. Quite the contrary. David was insisting that this sin of adultery was not his first sin. Many other sins and sinful thoughts came before this and led him step by step to this monstrous sin. It is as though he were saying, Lord, I do not remember when it all started. I have sinned as long as I can remember—all my life. I was born into a sinful world and am part of it. Lord, I am no better than this sinful world of sinners.

If this passage is taken to mean literally that David sinned from the moment of his birth, or before, then this would contradict the biblical use of the word *sin* as the willful turning away from God or the willful transgression of the will of God. God does not hold one responsible for what one cannot prevent. "Sin is not counted where there is no law" (Rom. 5:13). An infant cannot have any concept of right and wrong and is therefore not sinning at all.

This is why Christian theologians have insisted that if the word *sin* is applied to newborn infants in any way, it cannot include the concept of guilt. Guilt includes responsibility and responsibility requires knowledge. So if this passage is taken to mean that infants sin, it is unique in Scripture.

Notice carefully that we are not saying that this scripture is not true. We are not saying that it is false. We are not saying that David was wrong when he wrote this. We are simply seeking to understand what he meant to be saying and implying.

Scripture must always be interpreted in the light of other Scripture. A basic rule of biblical exegesis is that no passage must be interpreted in such a way that it contradicts other passages. Another basic rule is that difficult passages must always be interpreted in the light of simpler passages. This passage in Psalms is not simple. Some ways of understanding it would contradict much of the rest of the Bible. Those ways cannot be correct. We are duty-bound to seek to understand this passage in such a way that it harmonizes with what the rest of the Bible teaches. No Christian can afford to be shallow in his or her consideration of such a passage or simply to take the first idea that occurs to one as he or she reads it. No one has a right to insist on an interpretation of any passage if that interpretation does not harmonize with other clear biblical concepts.

This point of the proper interpretation of Scripture is imperative. I know how difficult it is for anyone to change his concept of the proper interpretation of a verse. I know how hard it is for me to do so. After I have thought that a passage has a particular meaning, it is not easy to see that any other meaning could possibly be correct. Yet if we study the Bible as we should, we shall all have to do this frequently. This is what Bible study is all about. We are naive to imagine that our first thought concerning the meaning of a text must be the truth, the whole truth, and nothing but the truth. Language is not that simple. And the Bible is not that simple. God gave us a book that can show the most simple-minded person the way to God and heaven but that is profound enough to challenge the greatest minds of all ages. Therefore we must continue searching for the truth God has made available and keep searching for more truth, even when we believe we have found it.

With this thought in mind, let us take a careful look at the New Testament passage that is often said to teach a common concept of original sin as inborn depravity, Adamic nature, or innate depravity.

Romans 5:12-14

Therefore as sin came into the world through one man and death through sin, and so death spread to all men because all men sinned—sin indeed was in the world before the law was given, but sin is not counted where there is no law. Yet death reigned from Adam to Moses, even over those whose sins were not like the transgression of Adam, who was a type of the one who was to come (Rom. 5:12-14).

This passage is the origin of the concept of Adamic nature or innate depravity. If this passage does not teach this, then the doctrine cannot be found in the Bible.

One way to examine the exact meaning of a passage is to

ask ourselves questions about the passage, as though we were directly questioning the author. For example, we may ask, Why do all human beings sin? But when we look closely at this passage, we see that Paul does not say why all human beings sin. His subject is not why all sin, but why all die. We ask again, What is the connection between the sin of Adam and my own sin? Again, Paul does not say, What effect does Adam's sin have on a baby's nature? Paul says nothing of this. Is Adam's sin imputed or charged to me? Nothing is said. Did I sin when Adam sinned? No. Did I become guilty of sin because Adam sinned? No. I only become guilty when I sin through my own choice. Am I born sinful or sinning because Adam sinned? Paul says nothing of this idea at all.

What, then, does Paul say? He simply says that Adam sinned and the death penalty was passed on sinners. Therefore all human beings die. Note that Paul does not seek to explain why all sin, but he simply says that all die because all sin. He assumes that we can see and know for sure that all sin, and he shows that this is the reason that all die.

Contradictory Interpretations

Because so much has been read into this passage in the past, we would be wise to look at some of the interpretations that have resulted from asking the passage to explicate what it does not discuss: Why do all sin? We will look especially at the three most strongly supported theories.

1. *A Neo-orthodox view.* Barth and Brunner have suggested that "each man is his own Adam." Just as Adam sinned, so each person sins, becomes depraved, and dies. What this amounts to is that there is no connection at all between Adam's sin and ours. It does not even matter in this case whether Adam ever sinned or even lived. In this view, Adam was a sort of mythical prototype of each person since and it is not necessary to know whether or not he really lived. The sin of Adam is only a sort of type of each person's sin and fall.

Such a concept does not appeal to those of us who take more seriously the historicity of all that the Bible records.

We can see that there is some truth in the idea that we are all sinners as Adam was. But Paul, in Romans 5:15-21, seems to take Adam more seriously than that. His comparison of Christ and Adam seems to require that Adam be as truly historical as Christ. So, although this interpretation may seem to express some truth about us, it does not seem to say enough and so must be rejected.

2. *An Augustinian view.* Pelagius, at the end of the fourth century, argued that each person came into the world perfectly free to live without ever sinning and capable of doing so. Each one is in the exact condition as Adam. One needs nothing more and can in his or her own power please God perfectly. This amounted to the conclusion that one does not need God's help to be saved but can save himself or herself. Certainly, this is pressing our human ability much too far.

Augustine was so disturbed about this teaching that he went to the opposite extreme and said that because of the sin of Adam, we are all born so depraved that we can do nothing at all toward our salvation. We are not even capable of responding to God's call for us to repent. We are totally depraved—through the sin of Adam—and thus totally unable to do anything good. More than one thousand years later, Calvin adopted and elaborated this view of Augustine's.

But Augustine, in rightly opposing Pelagius, went much too far to the opposite extreme, like a pendulum that swings from one extreme to another. One aspect of his teaching that is relevant at this point is that Augustine decided that all human beings were in some way in Adam when he sinned and that when he sinned, all sinned and became guilty before God. In this way, all are born into the world as guilty sinners and totally depraved by our own sin that we committed in Adam at the beginning. We are then unable to do anything good. We cannot even respond to God's call to repent and receive salvation.

This is what forced Augustine to invent the idea of irresistible, individual predestination. If we are totally incapable of responding to God, then it is impossible for anyone to get saved at all, unless God just decides whom to save, and then saves those persons, whether they want to be saved or not. He had talked himself into a blind alley and could think of no other way to account for the fact that some are saved, and some are not saved. So he put all the responsibility on the choice of God. In this he was unscriptural and wrong. He came to this conclusion, not from the study of the Bible teaching, but by reasoning from his own assumptions. Those assumptions were the result of his emotional reaction to the false concepts of Pelagius.

One problem with the teaching of Augustine is the way others have adopted this concept of the nature of humankind. So the biblical word *predestination* has come to mean "irresistible individual predestination." The biblical use of the word tends to be overlooked in favor of this later use. This makes it difficult to see just what the Bible teaches on this important point.

This is not the place to discuss the whole subject of predestination. The important point, however, is that the Augustinian concept of total depravity leads logically straight to the concept of irresistible personal predestination. Since the latter is not scriptural, the former could not logically be a Bible teaching either. The wrongness of the conclusion demonstrates the logical wrongness of the premise. So we have to reject the idea of total depravity inherited from Adam—if by total depravity we mean what Augustine meant by the term— total inability to do anything toward accepting God's offered salvation.

Note one more point about Augustine's teaching. Augustine read his concept of inherited guilt and total inability into Romans 5:12. In the Latin version he was using, he read "in whom (in quo) all sinned" He then applied the "whom" to Adam and said that in Adam all future persons sinned. Even Calvin rejected this exegesis of the verse as wrong, though he clung to Augustine's conclusions just the same, but without biblical support.

As Calvin pointed out, the Greek, *eph ho* is more accurately translated into Latin by *quia, quandoquidem.* In English, the idea is best expressed by something like "because," "since," or "in that." Paul seems to be saying simply that all die because all have sinned.

3. *Innate tendency to sin.* This concept states that we are born with an inheritance from Adam of some innate tendency to sin. This seems like a logical way of accounting for the universality of sin, but it is not what Paul said in Romans 5:12. This idea would hinder the thought of Paul here. Paul was not trying to explain why all sin, but why all die. His subject was not sin and salvation in this chapter and the next, but death and life.

Dr. Wilbur Dayton says of this passage:

This section is regarded by many as the most difficult passage in the New Testament. However, much of the difficulty is probably caused by reading into it views never intended by the Apostle . . . What Paul takes for granted as a basis to illustrate something else becomes, in their minds, the central argument. Then, having spent their energy on the assumed universality of sin, they seldom give equal attention to the real point of the passage—the supreme adequacy of redemption.[9]

Dr. Dayton continues by pointing out five things Paul did not say here, but which are often read into the passage by eisegesis:

a. Paul did not say that sin was imputed to all because of Adam's sin.

b. Paul does not say that all were present in Adam and sinned when Adam sinned.

c. He does not mention any preexistence of all in Adam, during which guilt was acquired by all.

d. He does not say that all die because Adam sinned. He said that all die because all sin. He says that the death penalty was passed on sinners because of Adam's sin.

e. Paul did not say why all sin. It seems, then, that it would be safer for us not to seek for the answer.

We can agree, then, that Romans 5 is not such a problem unless we ask of it a question that it does not answer, or even discuss. Paul did not seem to have any problem with the cause of the universality of sin, or he would not have taken it for granted here. He assumes that we all know that and will not argue about it. He then uses that as a basis for his reasoning about death.

The fact is that since we all are born into the world without a conscious knowledge of God and with no personal relationship with Him through the indwelling Holy Spirit, it is no wonder that we all sin. When we come to the age of responsibility, we choose to do our own will rather than God's will. We choose to exalt ourselves rather than God. We choose to do what we please.

When we add to this the prevalence of sin in the world and the temptations of Satan, we have no problem understanding why all sin. Who can resist sin without the power of the indwelling Holy Spirit? The wonder is that we are not all worse than we are. Whatever goodness there is in this sinful world is due to the work of the Holy Spirit in the hearts of sinners; for he is working in all to bring them to a saving knowledge of Christ and to prevent them, if possible, from going deeper into sin.

1 Corinthians 15:22

Besides Romans 5:12, this passage is often also used to support the idea of an inherited sinful nature coming from Adam. It reads, "For as in Adam all die, so also in Christ shall all be made alive."

The first thing to notice is that this is in the context of the great chapter on resurrection. The discussion is on the subject of the resurrection of Christ and the future resurrection of all at the Day of Judgment. So Paul is here discussing physical death and resurrection, not sin and salvation. Nothing is said of sin in this passage, but rather of death. For this reason, the idea of inheriting sinfulness from Adam could not have originated in the reading of this verse, if it had not already been read into Romans 5:12. This is why we have said that Romans 5:12 is the more important passage to be discussed on this point. We have seen that it does not teach that we inherit sin and guilt from Adam. However, we have seen that we are born less than holy because of Adam.

A Clearer View

By this time we may see that theological terms are used wrongly, such as *original sin, innate depravity, inherited sin* and even *holiness.* We need to see clearly what is wrong.

The basic problem is that these terms have been depersonalized in our thinking. These are all personal terms and cannot be understood biblically by impersonal thinking. We have seen previously that sin, for example, is committed by a person against a personal God. Sin is not a thing, but a choice of a person. Whether it is the choice of an act, desire, attitude, or disposition, it is the choice of a person against the Person God.

Sin, then, is the person turning away from God. It is not a thing within the person. It is the whole person turned in the wrong direction. William Temple dealt helpfully with this when he wrote about sin:

The center of the trouble is not the turbulent appetites, though they are troublesome enough, and the human faculty for imagination increases the turbulence. But the center of trouble is the personality as a whole, which is self-centered and can only be wholesome and healthy if it is God-centered. This whole personality in action is the will; and it is the will which is perverted."[10]

See how a personalized view of theology makes a difference in all aspects of theology. Nothing is more important to understand if we are to have a biblical view of sin and holiness. If sin is the orientation of the whole person away from God, then holiness is the whole person turned in love to God. It is not merely the absence of sin, but the presence of the God-given love for God. It is given by God, but can only be given when the person voluntarily chooses to respond to God's call to turn wholly to Him.

This understanding is what led Luther to prefer the term personal sin instead of original sin. And it makes sense out of the view of Arminius that original sin is deprivation rather than depravation. Actual sins of the individual bring about a depraved personality, but these sins grow out of the original deprivation of the person.

Wesley was close to the truth when he said so often that holiness is perfect love to God. Yet Wesley was all his life so bound by Augustine's view of sin and the Fall that he never quite found a consistent view of sanctification and holiness. He knew that sin was not a thing, and that there was no such thing as inherited guilt, yet at times he continued to speak of the removal of original sin. A better way is not far removed but makes a vast difference. That is to recognize both sin and holiness as relational, personal terms. This is the only way to think of sin and holiness in a consistently biblical way.

When we recognize that sin is not a thing, and that original sin is not an inherited substance, we can begin to see why the New Testament says nothing about the eradication of inborn depravity. It speaks instead of the Holy Spirit filling us with the love of God (Rom. 5:5) and of our yielding our "members to righteousness for sanctification" (Rom. 6:19). Instead of saying that we have no carnality (flesh) in us, Paul says that we "are not in the flesh" but "in the Spirit" (Rom. 8:9).

Some careful thought is required to make the change from a depersonalized theology to a personalized theology, but when this is accomplished, it becomes easier to make sense out of the teaching of the whole New Testament. One is no longer required to read so many ideas into the New Testament. One no longer has to infer that Paul had certain ideas that he did not express. But this can be seen more clearly as we look further at the concept of holiness.

Chapter 7:
Holiness as Personal
Relationship with God

L et us hope that we have not been looking so long at the
various aspects of sin that we have forgotten that our
primary object is to come to a better understanding of
holiness. We have been necessarily given careful consideration to the concept of sin, for it is one of the factors
determining the nature of holiness. We cannot know what
holiness is unless we understand what sin is. The two concepts are so closely interrelated that we must work on the
two together.

We have seen that sin is not a thing. Neither is holiness a
thing. Sin is the turning of the whole person away from God,
and holiness is the turning of the whole person in love to
God.

Holiness Is Positive

One of the basic concepts we must settle first of all is that
holiness is a positive relationship with God, and sin is the
lack of it. As light is a positive, and darkness is the absence
of light, so holiness is love for God, and sin is the absence of
it.

When we say this, we are speaking of sin as the basic orientation of the person away from God, and not of individual

acts of sin that follow from that wrong orientation of the soul. At this point perhaps it is time to clear up one of the common misunderstandings about sin. Sins are not simply isolated acts or attitudes that have no real relationship to one another. It is not that a person goes through life committing this sin now and another later on. The person who is not a Christian is living in sin, and his or her actions and attitudes are all interrelated. They are a part of his or her sinful character. They are all of a piece and not isolated events. He or she sins because the person is living in sin. The Christian is holy because he or she is living in Christ.

In a depersonalized world-view, people think of sins as isolated events. Sometimes we call this the "atomic" view of sin. That is, each sin is thought of as an atom, isolated from other sins. Such a view is not only unrealistic, psychologically unsound, and unscriptural, but it leads to a false concept of holiness, also.

If sin is isolated events, then holiness is seen to be impossible for human beings, since it is so easy for us to do something that is less than our best. We can then feel as though we have lost all the goodness and holiness we ever had and feel that the whole attempt to be holy is hopeless. But if holiness is perfect love to God and sin is the absence of that love, we have a far different situation. If holiness is being turned in love toward God, and sin is turning away from God, then surely we can know whether or not we still love God with all our hearts! We can know whether or not we have turned our hearts away from him. We can know his continued and continuing forgiveness of our failings. We can forgive ourselves more easily when we know that he forgives. "For he knows our frame; he remembers that we are dust" (Ps. 103:14).

This does not mean that we can casually go on living in sin and feeling that God forgives all we do. God forbid! It simply means that God knows what we can do by his grace and what we cannot do because of our human frailty, ignorance, or lack of maturity. God is at least as merciful with us as we parents are with little children. We do not expect them to act like adults, for we know that they cannot. We do not expect an infant to know better than to cry while the preacher is preaching. We do expect the child to learn—in time. But not yet. We do not scold the three-year-old for wanting to cross the street against the red light. We expect the child to learn this, but not to know it yet. If the little child brings a handful of weeds as a beautiful gift of love to us, we accept it as the loving gift it is and say nothing of the lack of beauty. We are happy for the love. We know that God can see the love in our hearts, even when our actions do not measure up to the standard of maturity he hopes to help us to attain in time.

Let us now return to the concept of holiness as positive value—positive love for God. Sin is real and most wicked. But holiness is positive, and sin is the lack of it. This is quite different from the usual way of thinking of sin as positive and holiness as the negative. If holiness is only the lack of sin, then holiness may seem very difficult, if not impossible. If holiness is the total absence of sin, then we must look very carefully at a person and his or her life before we dare to say that the person is holy. We must be very sure that some little sin somewhere in his or her life has not been overlooked.

The basic problem here is the logical impossibility of proving a universal negative. Suppose someone says, "No two snowflakes are exactly alike." That is a universal negative. But it cannot be proved by examining a thousand snowflakes. One would have to examine all the snowflakes that ever form in order to be sure that no two are alike. And the trouble with that is that no one can ever examine all of them. Most of them melt or are buried under others long before the most agile investigator could get to them. A positive statement would be better, such as, "The snowflakes come in such a bewildering variety of shapes and sizes that they all seem to be different from each other." This can be shown to be true by studying and photographing a thousand or so snowflakes.

It is the same with sin and holiness. If sin is positive, and holiness is the absence of sin, then how could anyone ever be so bold as to speak of human holiness? How could we be sure that some little sin had not been overlooked somehow?

What if we were wrong about something and did not know it? Could we ever be sure that we had lived totally without sin for any given period of time?

Clearly, this is all too common a concept of sin and holiness, however, causing no end of trouble and discouragement among Christians. Young Christians especially are tempted to give up the whole struggle as they learn that something they have been doing now is seen to be wrong, even though they did not know it at the time. This concept leads a person to feel that growth is too slow to do him or her any good. Actually, one cannot grow in the Lord without learning that one's past life has been less than perfect. Every parent knows what it is to look back and see how the training of the children could have been better accomplished. Every Christian knows what it is to look back and see how he or she could have done better at one point or another. That is the result of growing maturity, and it is a part of being a Christian.

The fact is that if holiness is simply the absence of sin, we are all too familiar with the imperfections of human beings. We make mistakes and blunders of all kinds. We spell words incorrectly use less-than-perfect grammar, forget names, drop things, stumble, and unintentionally hurt the feelings of others. Knowing full well that all human beings fail in these ways and a thousand others, we marvel at the statement of Jesus, "You, therefore, must be perfect, as your heavenly Father is perfect" (Matt. 5:48).

Perfect?

When asked what they think Jesus meant by this command, people give a variety of responses. One of the most common answers offered is that Jesus must have left out a word; he meant, "Try to be perfect." On first examination this seems to help a little, since we can all make it our aim or goal to be as near perfect as possible in everything. And surely, if we are trying to do right, God knows that and will reward sincere effort. God knows whether we are trying or not and will help us when we try. We must never be content

78

with less than our best. So the idea contains some truth that Jesus meant for us to be as nearly like God as we can. Yet this is not just what Jesus said.

Others take the Greek word *teleios* to mean "mature, full-grown, completely finished." But this seems to me to compound the problem. At what age do we become mature or completely finished? What good does it do to tell a fifteen-year-old convert to be mature? How can a person be mature when he or she is immature? For that matter, what good does it do to tell any of us to be completely finished?

We cannot be what we are not, just by being told to be that. When Jesus said for us to be perfect, he was talking about the love we have for others. He said that God showed love to all persons, whether they loved God or not. And he does. So Jesus told us that showing love to all, whether we are loved in return or not, is the way to be like God. It is not easy, but it can be done by the grace of God. This is what Jesus told us to do. Since this takes effort and prayer on our part, then we must try. But it can really be accomplished only by the grace of God as given to us by the Holy Spirit.

Fellowship with God

Before we explore further what it means to be like God, we need to consider the fact that the message of the whole Bible is that we are to love him and to have constant communion with him. God's plan did not wait for the coming of the Messiah for implementation. We find in the very beginning of the Old Testament that people knew God and had regular communion with him.

We know very little about Adam and Eve before the Fall, but we can infer that they had regular fellowship with God. Even after they had sinned, when they came to feel the presence of God in the garden, they recognized his presence and were ashamed of themselves for what they had done. Thus, they tried to hide themselves (Gen. 3:8). Then they easily recognized the voice of God when he spoke to them. This could only have come from regular communion with God.

We must also understand that the Holy Spirit was not created on the Day of Pentecost but was present from the beginning of creation and before. He is mentioned in Genesis 1:9 and was the same Holy Spirit who was sent to do a special work in the hearts of people beginning on the Day of Pentecost. So God spoke to Adam through the Holy Spirit just as he does to us today. One difference is that before Adam ever sinned, his heart had never been hardened, and he was more easily able to hear and recognize the Spirit. He had the perfect, unsullied spiritual ear to hear God speak through the Spirit.

It is said of Enoch (Gen. 5:22) and Noah (6:9) that they "walked with God." In the midst of all the sin and degradation after the Fall, these two people stand out as blessed by God with regular, daily fellowship with him. It is possible to live godly lives in this wicked world, as they proved even in that early, pre-Christian day of wickedness.

Then after all the growing wickedness leading up to the Flood and the strife around the Tower of Babel with the consequent scattering of the people, God somehow found Terah and Abram. He took them out of their wicked environment and taught them to live for him alone.

If we look through the rest of the history of the Old Testament, we see how God worked especially with certain persons in many ages to teach them to know him in an unusual close fellowship. This made it possible for such persons to become leaders in their generations and to show others the will of God more perfectly. All this was the work of the Holy Spirit in the hearts of people of the Old Testament. This seems strange to some good Christians who have been accustomed to thinking of the work of the Holy Spirit as beginning fifty days after the resurrection of Christ. But, of course, the Holy Spirit had been doing the same work for thousands of years. One difference is that in the Old Testament, he did for a few what he wills to do for all today. This is the point of the words of Jeremiah in the great passage about the new covenant when God said, "For they shall all know me, from the least of them to the greatest, says

80

the Lord" (Jer. 31:34).

So it is obvious that God's plan from the beginning of creation was to have a people with a special love-relationship with him, who would love and serve him, and with whom he could have constant close fellowship and communion. God has desired this, not at all because of human greatness or wisdom but simply because God chose to set his love upon us. He wants our love in return. He did not at all want robots who would do his will from necessity. He has longed for people with a free will to choose to love and serve him in response to his love for them. Sin wrecked this plan in the beginning, but God refused to give up. He determined to prepare the way, by the Holy Spirit, for the coming of Jesus Christ, who would make possible a plan of salvation from sin for those who would accept it.

This right relationship with God is the essence of holiness, just as a wrong relationship is the essence of sin. That this right relationship is one of love to God we will discuss later. Just now we need to see some of the requirements that must be met if we are to have a right relationship with God. These requirements are based on the very nature of God himself.

Holiness Based on God's Perfection

1. *As a holy being, God is perfect in righteousness.* "Shall not the Judge of all the earth do right?" (Gen. 18:25). If we are to be God's people, we must do righteously and not just talk about righteousness. We cannot casually excuse sin in ourselves and expect God to bless our desire for fellowship with him.

2. *As a holy being, God is perfect in his justice.* His commandments are perfectly fair. Each one is judged according to "what he has done in the body" (2 Cor. 5:10). At that last day, all shall be judged "by what they had done" (Rev. 20:13). God is perfectly fair to all in his judgment.

3. *As a holy being, God is perfect in his truthfulness.* "God is not man, that he should lie . . . Has he said, and will he not do it? Or has he spoken, and will he not fulfill it?" (Num. 23:19).

4. *As a holy being, God is perfect in his faithfulness.* "The steadfast love of the Lord never ceases, his mercies never come to an end; they are new every morning; great is thy faithfulness" (Lam. 3:22-23).

5. *As a holy being, God is perfect in his love.* Jesus put it strongly:

> But I say to you, Love your enemies and pray for those who persecute you, so that you may be the sons of your Father who is in heaven; for he makes his sun rise on the evil and on the good, and sends rain on the just and on the unjust. . . . You, therefore, must be perfect" (Matt. 5:44-45, 48).

This perfect love of God for all human beings is the reason God wants so much for us to love him in return. This amazing, incomprehensible love of God for us is the most astonishing idea we could imagine. We who have grown up hearing the Christian message do not realize how startling it is to read that "God is love." Other religions have no concept of a god of love. Even Jews do not understand this stress of the New Testament on the love of God for all. It is true that the Old Testament speaks of the love of God, and even of the love of God for the lost, but it is not stressed there as it is in the New Testament, and so it is easily overlooked. A rabbi who had just been studying the Gospels said that the most amazing thing he had read was the parable of the lost sheep (Luke 15:3-7). He could not imagine God actually going out to seek for the lost and bring them back to himself! Yet this is exactly what the message of the gospel is all about.

Our Love for God

Our love for God is in response to God's love for us. We did not seek for God; for he sought for us. Our search for God was a response to God's seeking us out. He sought us long before we sought for him. He loved us before we began to love him. God took the initiative in love. He loved us first, or we could not have learned to love him.

This is what John meant when he wrote, "We love, because he first loved us" (1 John 4:19). (It is true that the King James Version says "We love God," but the word *God* was probably a later addition, and not what John originally wrote.) We learn to love through being loved by God. We love God, and we love others, because he first loved us so very much.

God loved us when we were unlovely, and almost unlovable. God loved us, not because we were lovely, but because he is love.

As George Allen Turner wrote, "The Bible is concerned, not so much with the production of a perfect man, but union of that man with the perfection of God."[1]

It is God who is perfect, and we can never hope to be perfect in the same way or to the same degree. But we can have a perfect relationship of love with the perfect God of love, because that is what he chooses for us.

But what of the passages that speak of certain persons as "perfect" in the sight of God? Such persons as Noah, Abraham, and Job were called perfect in God's eyes. We know for sure that it could not be said of any of these that they never made a mistake in their whole lives, so that is not what is meant. How could God call them perfect?

What we have to say is that these persons were perfect in their love for God. They may not have expressed this love perfectly. They sometimes blundered as they attempted to do God's will. But they loved God so that they did make the attempt. When they failed, they sought God's forgiveness, so that they could go on trying to live with and for God. Thus they carried on the adventure of holiness.

A little child may love his or her parents very much, even though the child does not always know good ways of demonstrating that love. Children may be more a hindrance than a help as they try to do something good for their parents out of pure love. But the parent knows the love behind the act, and understands that the action which is less than perfect expresses perfect love. The child will grow and love but is now doing all that we can expect from a child of that age and ability. The parent can then call that child perfect, in spite of the imperfections. The infant who makes a mess of the room trying to feed itself is called perfect by the parents because of the attempt at such a young age. So it is that God, who made us, and who knows our hearts, who understands our lack of knowledge and understanding, calls us perfect when he knows that what we do is done out of unsullied love for him.

In this sense, our human perfection must be called relative perfection, in contrast with the absolute perfection of God. Relative perfection is all that any human being can ever have, for only the infinite God can be absolutely perfect in anything.

Yet relative perfection is real perfection. The fact is that the word *perfect* always means relatively perfect when applied to anything but to God, as all large dictionaries explain. Human beings could not define, describe, or recognize absolute perfection in anything. When we call a line "perfectly straight" we know that it is not absolutely perfect in straightness. Any microscope will show that it is not even a line, since it varies in width, and a line has no width at all. What we draw simply represents a straight line. Some lines are better representations than others, but judged by absolute standards, they are not lines at all and are far from perfect. Yet if they are straight enough for our purpose we can call them "perfect."

Here, then, is the clue to the meaning of perfection. To call anything perfect means that it is "good enough for the purpose for which it is to be used." Or that it "meets the standards of the maker." It may not be good enough for other purposes and may not meet the standards of some other person, but it is perfect if it measures up to the standards of the maker or user.

What the Christian must do is to meet the standards of the Creator God for that particular person. God judges each person individually. God knows the heart, the mind, the soul, the body of that person and does not expect more of anyone than that person can do at that time. God does expect us to learn and grow. But at any particular time, God knows just what is reasonable. God knows us better than we know ourselves and far better than we can ever know others.

A caution: we must judge ourselves far stricter than we judge others. This is why Jesus warned us:

Judge not, that you be not judged. For with the judgment you pronounce you will be judged, and the measure you give will be the measure you get (Matt. 7:1-2).

The Christian will not presume on the love and mercy of God but will regret any failure so that he or she begs for forgiveness. We cannot simply overlook failure and depend on the love of God to forgive automatically. We must ask and plead for forgiveness and seek not to fail again in that same way. This is the way of growth. This is the way to keep the path clear between the soul and God. This is the way to continue walking in the highway of holiness. This is the adventure of holiness.

Love for God

We have been insisting that holiness is a positive rather than a negative. Holiness is positive love for God. Holiness itself is not the leaving off of things, or actions. It may require us to leave off some things, but that is not the essence of holiness. We drop off things because of our love for God. This love for God is the essence of holiness and not the mere fact that we have omitted some things. Understanding this will give us a more exciting, effective, and dynamic concept of holiness.

Growing up in a preacher's home, I heard some of the best and some of the poorest of preachers. All my life as a boy I went to camp meetings, revivals, and ministers meetings, and I sat through all the services. I must admit I heard a lot of negative preaching on holiness in some of those services. Good men and women preached on holiness, but all too often the stress was on what must be left off. Sometimes holiness seemed like a dreary business. However, I must hasten to add that this was not my major impression. Partly because of my own parents, who were both ordained ministers, and partly because of some of the more godly and more balanced preachers I knew, I came to understand that holiness in not primarily negative. My father was especially strong on this point, and as I grew older, he sometimes pointed out to me the fallacy of some of the negative emphasis in the preaching we had heard. How thankful I am for that. I came to see that holiness is not inhuman or impossible, but a wonderful walk with God, made possible by his love and mercy to us.

Chapter 8:
Victory Over Sin

For sin will have no dominion over you, since you are not under law but under grace.—Rom. 6:14

We Christians do not have to live in constant guilt. God does not plan for us to live in sin all through this life, wishing we could do better, but knowing that we cannot. We can live in this present world lives that are pleasing to God because of our love for God in response to his love for us. What a blessing it is for us to be able to say with Paul:

There is therefore now no condemnation for those who are in Christ Jesus. For the law of the Spirit of life in Christ Jesus has set me free from the law of sin and death (Rom. 8:1-2).

This passage from Paul is totally contrary to the common idea that no one can live in victory over sin in this world. The almost universal belief is that we cannot live in the world without sinning all the time. This concept is clearly expressed in the Westminster Catechism:

No man even by the aid of Divine grace, can avoid sinning, but daily sins in thought, word and deed.

But if this is true, what is the difference between a sinner and a Christian? What is the advantage of being a Christian? We would have to say, then, that the Christian sins as much as the sinner, but that the Christian is automatically forgiven for all his sins as he commits them. Or is he forgiven ahead of time for all the sins he is going to commit?

If it is true that no one is able to live one day without sinning "in thought, word and deed, even with the help of the Holy Spirit and all grace of heaven" then the plan of salvation must be a total failure. Jesus came to "save his people from their sins." But if we go on sinning every day, how can we be said to be "saved from sin?"

What we need to do is look at what the New Testament actually says about the Christian and sin.

Dead to Sin

Romans 6 states as clearly as can be done in human language that the Christian has died to sin and must not live in sin any longer.

> What shall we say then? Are we to continue in sin that grace may abound? By no means! How can we who died to sin still live in it? (Rom. 6:1-2).

He is surely speaking of himself and all of his fellow-Christians when he says "we who died to sin." If we have died to sin, how can we continue to live in it? This is the question. The answer is that we cannot continue to live if we are dead. If we are dead to sin, we cannot go on living in it. Just as Christ died on the cross, so we have died to sin, and as he rose from the grave, so we can rise to "walk in newness of life" (v. 4). "For if we have been united with him in a death like his, we shall certainly be united with him in a resurrection like his" (v. 5).

This seems perfectly clear, but some are not willing to accept the conclusion that the Christian can therefore live in victory over sin. J. Sidlow Baxter, in *A New Call to Holiness*, creates a complicated theory based on the interpretation that when Paul says we died with Christ, he means that that death took place at Calvary, but that we can never in this world experience a death to sin that makes holiness possible. Baxter claims that Paul is speaking of legal matters, not experiential. He is speaking of dying to law, not dying to sin in actuality.[1] But this cannot be supported. Paul clearly said, "How can we who died to sin. . . ." He plainly means dying to sin, and continuing to live in sin.

Further, in verses 6-7, Paul plainly states:

> We know that our old self was crucified with him so that the sinful body might be destroyed, and we might no longer be enslaved to sin. For he who has died is freed from sin.

So Paul is clearly speaking of death to sin, no longer being enslaved to sin, freed from sin. He is not speaking here, as in Romans 7:1-6, of dying to the Law, but of dying to sin, as he says.

So the Christian has died to the power of sin and must not go on living in sin. "So you also must consider yourselves dead to sin and alive to God in Christ Jesus" (v. 11). Here we see the strange paradox that Paul often tells the Christian to be what he is. You are dead to sin, therefore be dead to sin. Consider yourself dead to sin. You are holy; therefore be holy!

The Christian must be warned against forgetting what he or she is. The Christian must struggle to keep what he or she has gained in Christ. As Jesus put it, "But he who endures [goes on enduring] to the end will be saved" (Matt. 24:13). As one must accept salvation by faith, so one must persist, by faith, in living a life worthy of the gospel he or she has received (Eph. 4:1). Paul, then, uses both the indicative and the imperative. You are dead to sin; therefore be dead to sin. Count yourself dead to sin, because you are. Keep on considering yourself dead to sin, since you are dead to sin.

The Christian is dead to sin, but he or she is not dead to temptation. No one is safe who forgets that. We do not have to sin, but we do have to be tempted, as long as we are living in this world. Jesus was tempted in all the ways in which we are tempted (Heb. 4:15; Matt. 4; and others), so we must not expect to get beyond the point of temptation. We will be tempted as long as we are physically and mentally alive; but we do not have to sin. We can be tempted severely, yet without sinning, by the power and grace of God.

So the fact is that we cannot help being tempted, but we do not have to yield to temptation. We do not have to sin.

Consider what it means to be "dead to sin." Jesus had said that "every one who commits sin is a slave to sin" (John 8:34). A slave must go on working as a slave as long as she or he is alive. When a slave dies, she or he is no longer bound to the owner. If we sin, we are slaves to sin. But when we die to sin, we are no longer in bondage to sin. We are no longer bound to our former owner and no longer have to obey. We do not have to sin. So Paul states that we died to sin, so that "we might no longer be enslaved to sin" (Romans 6:6). The bondage to sin has come to an end. The power of sin no longer enslaves us.

If we are dead to sin, does this mean that we automatically live blameless lives? Does it mean that we cannot sin anymore? If we have died to sin, is it no longer possible for us to commit sin? Do we lose our freedom of choice when we die to sin, so that we can no longer choose to sin?

Holiness preachers have never said these things, but opponents of holiness have often said them. They say that if we were really dead to sin, sin would be impossible for us to anymore. But this is not at all true. God does not make sinning impossible for us. But God does make it possible for us not to sin. God's Holy Spirit gives the Christian grace to resist temptation. He makes it possible for the Christian to keep his or her eyes fixed on Jesus and to live a life, by the grace of God, that pleases God.

It is never easy, very long at a time, to live a clean life, pure from sin. But it is possible. Temptation will sometimes be fierce and will often catch us unawares. It may often be like a constant battle, or an uphill struggle, to resist temptation and grow more and more like Christ, as we should. But it is not always like that. There are lulls in the battle and level places in our climb, so that we can catch our breath and be ready for the next struggle. God is with us and by his grace we can win. We do not depend on our own strength but on God's power.

The possibility of living without sin by the grace of God brings with it the necessity of holy living. If we can, then we must. So Paul concludes,

> Let not sin therefore reign in your mortal bodies, to make you obey their passions. Do not yield your members to sin as instruments of wickedness, but yield yourselves to God as men who have been brought from death to life, and your members to God as instruments of righteousness. For sin will have no dominion over you, since you are not under law but under grace (Rom. 6:12-14).

Since we no longer have to sin, then we are under obligation to live free from sin, by the grace of God. We are free from the power of sin, so we must yield our whole selves to our new Master and serve God with all our God-given abilities. This is our Christian obligation. Since it is possible, it is necessary. Since God gives us grace to overcome sin, he requires us to overcome.

> Once by sin our souls were bound
> And no helping hand we found,
> And we struggled for our freedom but in vain;
> Till our blessed Savior came,
> Washed away our guilt and shame,
> Gave us grace and help o'er sinfulness to reign.
>
> Sin shall not have dominion over you,
> For the Lord has spoken, and its power is broken,
> Sin shall not have dominion over you,
> For he causes us to triumph day by day.[2]
> —C. W. Naylor

Cleansed from All Sin

A passage that is always brought up when we talk about living without sinning is 1 John 1:8, "If we say we have no sin, we deceive ourselves, and the truth is not in us." Sometimes verse 10 is also quoted: "If we say we have not sinned, we make him a liar, and his word is not in us." It is not uncommon to hear a discussion on living without sinning in which someone quotes, "He that saith he liveth and sinneth not, is a liar, and the truth is not in him." That is a strong argument and I have often been asked how to answer it. But the answer is simple. There is no such scripture in the whole Bible. That last was just a misquotation of verses 8 and 10 quoted above.

Even so, the verses from 1 John 1 seem to be puzzling to many. What do they mean? Is John saying that it is impossible for anyone to live without sinning? No. These verses must be considered in their context, and we must not forget that they are joined together by verse 9. Look first at the context. In verse 5, John declares that "God is light and in him is no darkness at all." God and darkness simply do not mix. They are opposites. This leads John to say that we cannot walk with God while walking in darkness. We can do one or another, but not both. "But if we walk in the light, as he is in the light, we have fellowship with one another, and the blood of Jesus his Son cleanses us from all sin." It is at this point that John makes the statement in verse 8, "If we say we have no sin, we deceive ourselves." That is, if we say we have no sin from which to be cleansed, we are deceiving ourselves. If we say we do not need salvation, because we have never sinned, we are liars and the truth is not in us. But if we acknowledge our sin, we can be cleansed from it. So verse 9 says plainly, "If we confess our sins, he is faithful and just, and will forgive our sins and cleanse us from all unrighteousness." Then, to make the point very clear, John continues, "If we say we have not sinned, we make him a liar, and his word is not in us" (v. 10).

So the point of this passage is that we have all sinned before coming to God for salvation, but that when we admit this and repent of our sins, God does faithfully forgive them and cleanse us from all sin. John Wesley summed it up this way:

[It is] as if he had said, "I have before affirmed, 'the blood of Jesus Christ cleanseth us from all sin'; but let no man say, I need it not; I have no sin, to be cleansed from. If we say, that we have no sin, that we have not sinned, we deceive ourselves and make God a liar; but 'if we confess our sins, he is faithful and just,' not only to 'forgive our sins,' but also 'to cleanse us from all unrighteousness'; that we may 'go and sin no more.'[3]

That last statement by Wesley is a reference to the fact that twice when Jesus healed someone, he said to the person, "Sin no more" (John 5:14; 8:11). It would be totally incomprehensible for Jesus to say such a thing, if it were truly not possible for anyone in this life to live without sinning. But Jesus did say it, which is a clear indication that it is not impossible. We can live in this world without sinning. The expression used by Jesus (*meketi hamartane*) could properly be translated, "No longer go on sinning," or "Stop sinning." This is what one must do, by the grace of God, in order to be a Christian. Both Jesus and John made this clear in their teaching. But since 1 John has been interpreted in such different ways by some people, we will have to study certain other key passages in this book.

But If One Sins

Immediately after the statement we considered above, "If we say we have not sinned." John continues,

My little children, I am writing this to you so that you may not sin; but if any one does sin, we have an advocate with the Father, Jesus Christ the righteous; and he is the expiation for our sins, and not for ours only but also for the sins of the whole world (1 John 2:1-2).

Note that John insists that he is writing to show us that we should not sin. If we belong to God, then we ought to live without sinning. If he has cleansed us from all sin, then sin has no place in our hearts or lives. In this he is agreeing perfectly with what Jesus had said in John 5:14 and 8:11. He is saying that we must not sin. This is God's plan for us—that we live without sinning.

But what if we do fall into sin? What if we find that something we have done is sinful? Should we just forget it and go on as though it had not happened? No. For John has just been explaining that sin has no place in the life of the Christian. Sin must not be ignored. Should we give up and say that living without sin is too hard? Should we quit and say that it may be all right for others but that it does not work for us? Should we just admit that we are failures? No, for "we have an advocate with the Father." The same Jesus Christ who forgave our sins in the first place can forgive this sin and help us to go on in victory once more.

Here is one of the greatest problems for many young Christians. If they are rightly taught that we ought to live without sinning, they wonder what is wrong with them when they find sin in their lives. Realizing that they have fallen short of their God-given goal, they feel that since they have failed, they must be doomed to be failures. At this point the young Christian can go in one of two directions—both wrong. One can decide that the Christian life is impossible and give up the struggle. Or one can decide that something is wrong with the idea of living a holy life, a life without sinning. Either way, a person has lost something precious and wonderful. Either way one becomes a failure to oneself. This is tragic.

If we decide that, while others can live a holy life, we cannot, then the sense of failure is so strong that we can never again feel good about ourselves. We then sadly give up the attempt, and wonder what was wrong that God would not give the victory over sin. I have known some who have done this and gone on to church, living good lives, but afraid to claim salvation. I have known others who came to this point of failure and gave up all pretense of religion, turned away from the church, and went deeply into sin. Either way, a tragic, life-long sense of failure is sensed from which one cannot escape. This is just the opposite of what God has planned for each of us. He wants us to live in this world in victory over sin, rejoicing in the salvation of the Lord Jesus Christ.

So if one does find that he or she has sinned, the person is not to give up. John states clearly that "we have an advocate with the Father." That is, God still loves us and the blood of Jesus Christ can still cover sin. So the one who has sinned should immediately go to God and ask for forgiveness. Just as God forgave us before, he will forgive us now. We must never let sin go unforgiven or we can be lost. Instead, we must be sure to keep nothing between us and God by asking forgiveness immediately. It is far better to ask forgiveness for what is not really a sin, than to let sin go on unforgiven. It is better to be too conscientious than not conscientious enough. It is wiser to ask for forgiveness for careless mistakes or failings than to fail to ask often enough. Better safe than sorry. This way one does not have to decide each time whether or not this act was really sinful before deciding what to do about it. Simply ask forgiveness, accept it, and go on your way rejoicing in God's grace.

The Christian does not have to be defeated by sin. As John states, the plan of God for us is that we live without sinning at all. But even if we do fall into sin or find ourselves falling short of God's will for us, we still do not have to be defeated. We can call on God to forgive and know for sure that he does. We can then go on in the sure knowledge that God loves us, and we love him with all our hearts. Sin can have no power over us, unless we give in to it. We can live in constant victory and rejoice in the grace and love of God that makes this victory possible.

This victory we have, of course, is not in our own strength, but in the grace and strength of God alone.

The victory is mine, the victory is mine
Through Jesus my Lord, obeying his Word;
He conquers the foe wherever I go,
I'm living with him in holy accord.
                    —Barney E. Warren

95

Sin Is Lawlessness

In 1 John 3 the Apostle makes some strong statements about sin and the Christian and states clearly that the Christian does not go on sinning. In verse nine, he states plainly, "No one born of God commits sin; for God's nature abides in him, and he cannot sin because he is born of God." This strong statement has puzzled some because they have understood it to mean that the Christian is beyond the possibility of falling from grace and doing anything sinful. Or they feel that John must be stating some mysterious ideal but not speaking about ordinary persons. Others have concluded that the Christian can sin more or less but cannot make a habit of sinning. By this reasoning one can take all the meaning out of the verse and say that the Christian sins, but not as much as he or she used to.

The clue to the understanding of this verse lies in verse 4, where John begins this discussion by defining sin. "Every one who commits sin is guilty of lawlessness; sin is lawlessness." The Greek word for lawlessness is *anomia*, which signifies rebellion against law, or the conscious refusal to obey the law. It is the conscious refusal to do what one knows one ought to do. It presupposes a knowledge of the law or will of God, and an unwillingness to perform it. Sin, then, is "the willful transgression of the known will of God," as Wesleyans have traditionally described it.

John, then, has so defined sin that it has no place in the heart and life of any Christian. How can one be a born-again Christian, loving God with all his or her heart, and at the same time be refusing to do the will of God? This contradiction cannot be. Either one loves God and strives to do his will, or one does not truly love God and does not try to do his will.

After so defining sin as lawlessness, John says that Christ appeared "to take away sins" (v. 5), and then says plainly that "no one who abides in him sins" (v. 6). That is, no one who goes on abiding in Christ goes on committing sins— rebelling against God. The two things simply cannot exist together in the same heart.

The rest of verse 6 states the same truth in the obverse: "No one who sins has either seen him or known him." Does this mean that one who commits a sin has never been saved? Some have felt this to be true, but this is a misunderstanding. To say this, John would have had to use different tenses in the Greek. Even in this English translation one can easily see that it means at least that one who is now committing sins is not now a child of God. Does it go further and say that he never was a child of God? No. The two Greek verbs translated "has seen" and "has known" are in the Greek perfect tense. This tense signifies not what has happened in the past, but the present results of past action. In other words, John is saying that the one who is now living in sin is not now knowing and seeking God. No one can live in rebellion against God and at the same time live in personal communion with him. One either loves God and obeys him, or rebels against him and does not obey him. One cannot do both at the same time.

Now when we return to verse 9, we are in a position to understand it more clearly.

> No one born of God commits sin; for God's nature abides in him, and he cannot sin because he is born of God. By this it may be seen who are the children of God, and who are the children of the devil: whoever does not do right is not of God, nor he who does not love his brother (1 John 3:9-10).

We are not saying that one who is born of God finds sin it impossible to commit. But one cannot sin and at the same time be a child of God. Sin and rebellion simply cannot exist with love for God. Sin and love have nothing in common. A real change has taken place when a person becomes a child of God, and she or he cannot go on being the kind of rebel she or he was before.

All this is consistent with what John had said in 1:6: "If we say we have fellowship with him while we walk in darkness, we lie and do not live according to the truth." We cannot be walking in darkness and walking in light at the same time. We cannot be abiding in Christ and living in rebellion against him at the same time.

What we must keep in mind is the fact that sin is in the will and the purpose rather than in the act. Of course the act is wrong, but so is the purpose of doing the act. Sin begins long before the act of sin is ever performed. Jesus made that clear when he insisted that murder is wrong, but that one who hates another is also sinning (Matt. 5:21-26). He also insisted that adultery is sin, but that lust is also sin (Matt. 5:27-30). "Ethical writers insist that guilt always involves a knowledge of wrong, and an intention to commit it."[4] The intention is sin, even if the act is never committed. Without the intention or the motivating desire, the act itself may not bear real guilt. For example, if a surgeon causes the death of another person while seeking to save the life, the surgeon is not guilty. He sought only to do good. On the other hand, if one hates another and allows that hatred to fester and grow, one is guilty of sin even if no actual harm has been done. This is what is meant by saying that sin lies in the will and purpose and not primarily in the act.

Yet how easily we deceive ourselves. We can persuade ourselves that there is no sin in the heart, even though it is not true. How easily we say that we love God with the whole heart, even when the life does not support this. John knew this and that is why he said, "Little children, let no one deceive you. He who does right is righteous, as he is righteous" (3:7). It is not the person who says the most about his or her love for God who is righteous, but the one who shows his or her love by obedience to what he or she knows of the will of God.

Victory That Overcomes

Jesus announced to his disciples that he had "overcome the world" (John 16:33). He promised that those who believe in him can also be overcomers. Not surprisingly John takes up this same theme:

By this we know that . . . we love God and obey his commandments. For this is the love of God, that we keep his commandments. And his commandments are not burdensome. For whatever is born of God overcomes the world; and this is the victory that overcomes the world, our faith. Who is it that overcomes the world but he who believes that Jesus is the Son of God? (1 John 5:2-5).

By faith we can be overcomers. By faith we can overcome the world of sin, of evil, and of our former rebellion against the will of God. By faith we can overcome anything and everything that would hinder our constant fellowship with God in Christ Jesus. By faith we can have the victory over sin in our own hearts and lives. What a glorious thought this is, that we can be victors in all the fight against evil and sin. We do not have to be enslaved by sin any longer, but can live lives in this present world of victory, by faith in God.

The theme of the Book of Revelation is the battle between right and wrong, the battle between God and the devil, but that is not the whole theme. The rest of it is that the devil and wrong cannot triumph. God will win in the end. The devil is already a defeated enemy. He knows that his time is short. Christians have nothing to fear so long as they keep their trust in God, who will conquer all—with no possibility of failure. And not only that, but God has promised that we can be victorious in the struggle.

In the second and third chapters of this Book of Revelation there are letters from Christ to the seven representative churches of Asia Minor. Each of the letters ends with a promise to the person who overcomes sin in this life. Look at them:

To him who conquers I will grant to eat of the tree of life, which is in the paradise of God (2:7).

He who conquers shall not be hurt by the second death (2:11).

He who conquers and who keeps my works until the end, I will give him power over the nations . . . and I will give him the morning star (2:26, 28).

He who conquers shall be clad thus in white garments, and I will not blot his name out of the book of life; I will confess his name before my Father and before his angels (3:5).

He who conquers, I will make him a pillar in the temple of my God; never shall he go out of it, and I will write on him the name of my God . . . and my own new name (3:12).

He who conquers, I will grant him to sit with me on my throne, as I myself conquered and sat down with my Father on his throne (3:21).

Not only are these glorious promises given to those who conquer sin in this life by the grace of God, but we have the assurance of God in his Word that we can each have the victory in Christ Jesus. Not a single text in the New Testament which says that sin must remain in us until death. There is no hint that we must go on in slavery to sin all our lives long. We are told that we can have the victory over sin in this present world.

For the grace of God has appeared for the salvation of all men, training us to renounce irreligion and worldly passions, and to live sober, upright, and godly lives in this world, awaiting our blessed hope, the appearing of the glory of our great God and Savior Jesus Christ, who gave himself for us to redeem us from all iniquity and to purify for himself a people of his own who are zealous for good deeds (Titus 2:11-14).

The whole New Testament rings with a sense of freedom from sin. Its emphasis is on the victory of Calvary and on the grace of God that is able to give each of us the constant victory for which we ought to long with all our hearts. Sin must not reign over us and in us. Christ Jesus reigns in every heart that is surrendered to him in faith.

Jesus assured Pilate that he was King, but that his kingdom was not of this world. It is in the world, but not of the world. We are reigning in this life—reigning over sin in this present world. We do not have to do the will of Satan, as God can give us constant and complete victory over sin and temptation. We will continue to be tempted in many ways all through this life, but we do not have to yield to temptation—ever. And if we do, we are not defeated, for we have an Advocate with the Father—Jesus. Just as God forgave us when he first saved us, he will forgive us anytime we need it and give us ongoing victory so long as we continue to go on abiding in him.

When I was a boy growing up in the Church of God, I used to hear Christians greet one another with the question, "Do you have the victory?" The answer hoped for was a spontaneous "Yes!" But it was more often something like "Yes, Praise the Lord!" or something similar. This was not a bad custom. Do you have the victory?

Chapter 9:
The Spirit of Holiness

But the Counselor, the Holy Spirit, whom the Father will send in my name, he will teach you all things, and bring to your remembrance all that I have said to you (John 14:26)

W hen Jesus promised to send another Helper like himself, he called him the Holy Spirit. Who is this Holy Spirit? Why do we call him the Holy Spirit? Is this divine spirit simply some impersonal power or force in the universe? Why do we use personal pronouns for the Spirit, like he and him? What is the difference between the Holy Spirit and the Father and Son? We know about God the Father, and we know about Jesus Christ; what can we know about the Holy Spirit and his work?

We believe in the Father, and we believe firmly in Jesus Christ. Yet the Holy Spirit is just as much God as the other two members of the Trinity and is just as important. We need to understand what we can of him and his work, just as we need to understand the work of Jesus Christ in dying and rising again for our salvation from sin.

The Spirit Is God

In the New Testament, the words of God are quoted as being the words of the Holy Spirit, showing that the Spirit is

God. For example, in Isaiah 6:9 we read some words that God spoke to the prophet, and in Acts 28:25, Paul quotes these words and introduces them by saying, "The Holy Spirit was right in saying to your fathers through Isaiah the prophet. . . ." And when the words of God in Jeremiah 31:31 and following are quoted in Hebrews 10:15-17, he begins by saying, "And the Holy Spirit also bears witness to us; for after saying. . . ." So the word of God is regularly quoted as being the word of the Spirit. So the Holy Spirit must be God.

The terms *Spirit* and *God* are often used interchangeably in the New Testament. Believers are the temple of God, because the Spirit of God dwells in them. "A holy temple in the Lord; in whom you also are built into it for a dwelling place of God in the Spirit" (Eph. 2:21-22. cf. also 1 Cor. 6:19). In Romans 8:9, the Spirit of Christ is called the Spirit of God. Also in Acts 5:14, Peter told Ananias that he had lied to God in lying to the Holy Spirit.

The fact is that all through the Old and New Testaments, the Holy Spirit is spoken of as being God. He is as much God as the Father is God, or the Son. He was present and working in the creation of all things (Gen. 1:2). He is spoken of in divine terms all through the Old Testament, although he is only twice referred to as the "Holy Spirit." (The latter term is primarily found in the New Testament.)

Perhaps it ought to be mentioned here that some of the older translations referred to him as both "Holy Spirit" and "Holy Ghost." The two terms are used interchangeably. In fact, there is no reason for using both terms, since both are translations of the Greek word *Pneuma*. Possibly there was a desire for variety. But since the word *ghost* has taken on some undesirable connotations in English, it is perhaps better now to use only the one word *Spirit*. It will be noted that most modern versions follow this practice and for good reason. Using both words has given some the feeling that the Holy Spirit must be different from the Holy Ghost, but that is not true at all.

The Spirit Is Personal

The Holy Spirit is not a thing, but a personal being. One should never speak of the Holy Spirit as "it." He is personal, just as the Father and Son are personal. Theologians thus speak of them as three persons. They do not mean by this that they are human persons, but that they are not impersonal. God has all the good qualities that human personalities have, but in infinite quality. God can reason, choose, love, and so on, just as human beings can. In fact, we have these qualities, in limited degree, because God gave them to us. God wanted us to be enough like him to be able to know and love him and to serve him in love. The Holy Spirit, being God, is personal, not impersonal. He is not merely a force, or the power of God, but a thinking, reasoning, loving member of the Divine Trinity on the same level with God the Father and God the Son.

The personality of the Holy Spirit is shown in many ways by the Bible, especially in the New Testament. We have already seen that the Spirit is always referred to by the personal pronouns he and him, rather than it. We see further that we are baptized "in the name of" the Spirit, just as we are baptized "in the name of the Father and of the Son" (Matt. 28:19). Such a statement could only be made of a personal being, not a thing. When Paul concluded his second letter to Corinth with a blessing, he included the Holy Spirit: "The grace of the Lord Jesus Christ and the love of God and the fellowship of the Holy Spirit be with you all" (2 Cor. 13:14). Here again the personhood of the Spirit is shown.

The personhood of the Spirit is shown in the fact that he feels love. "I appeal to you, brethren, by our Lord Jesus Christ and by the love of the Spirit" (Rom. 15:30). This is the love of God that he pours into our hearts "through the Holy Spirit, which has been given to us" (Rom. 5:5). He can feel grief at our stubbornness or rebellion (Eph. 4:30). He sent Barnabas and Paul on their missionary tours (Acts 13:4) but would not at one time permit them to preach in Asia or Bithynia (Acts 16:6, 7). He told Paul that he was to undergo

105

imprisonment and afflictions in Jerusalem (Acts 20:23). Jesus promised that he would *abide* with us, or make his home in us (John 14:16); teach us (v. 26); bear witness of Christ (John 15:26); convince the world (16:8); and guide us (v. 13). He witnesses (Rom. 8:16); sanctifies (1 Cor. 6:11; Rom. 15:16), inspires (2 Pet. 1:21), and in many places is said to speak to and through people.

Perhaps the strongest illustration of his personality lies in the fact that sin against him is unpardonable (Matt. 12:31). This passage has led to much anguish on the part of some honest people who feel that they have sinned against the Holy Spirit and can never be saved. In most cases, that is not true. In fact, we can be certain that if a person is concerned about having committed this sin, he or she has not! The context of this remark by Jesus shows why he said it. When Jesus had cast out demons from a man and healed him, the Pharisees said that he did it by the power of the chief demon. But Jesus warned them that they were calling the Holy Spirit a demon. If they really decided that God is a devil, then there is was no way they could ever be saved. That would be to cut themselves off from the Holy Spirit, who is the only means of salvation. It would be like a person who had fallen into a well and cut off the only rope by which he could be pulled out. The fact is that anyone who puts off salvation until death has sinned against the Holy Spirit, who has sought to bring the person to Christ, and can never be saved. How dangerous it is to reject the wooing of the Holy Spirit by refusing to be saved!

The importance of this concept of the Spirit as a person cannot be easily overemphasized. The Spirit is not a thing that can be put inside of us or taken out. He is not something which we can possess and control as we control our physical possessions that belong to us. He is rather a person with whom we have a living, vital, personal relationship. Such a relationship is a growing one, in which we learn from him and grow in the grace and love he gives us. He leads, and we follow. He teaches, and we learn. He guides, and we know the way. He strengthens, and we are able to do all he chooses for us.

106

The Personal Helper

In John 14:16, we find the longest discussion of the Holy Spirit in the whole Bible. This was the last discourse of Jesus with his disciples before he was crucified the next morning. In it he spoke to them about the fact that he would soon be leaving them, but that he would send them another "helper" like himself to be with them in his stead. The Greek word Jesus used for the Spirit was *Paracletos*. The word is difficult to translate into English and has caused difficulties to translators for centuries. Some have simply transliterated the word to *Paraclete*. The King James Version uses *Comforter*, which used to have the right meaning (making one strong) but which now gives the wrong impression of what Jesus was saying. The Revised Standard Version usually uses "Counselor." This is close, but the Greek word has a broader meaning than this. Other terms that have been suggested are *Strengthener, Helper, Advocate,* and *Convincer.* I like the word "Helper" myself, although I understand the arguments against it. Leon Morris, for example, says that helper is not a good translation, since it is grammatically active, and *parakletos* is passive in meaning. However, this is only true etymologically. That is, the word *parakletos* was originally passive, but before the time of the New Testament it was being used actively, as it always is in the New Testament. So I like to use the word *Helper* in these chapters. It will not mislead us so long as we remember that the Spirit helps us in many different ways.

1. *He is our personal strengthener.* He will give us strength to do whatever it is the will of God for us to do. We will never be left entirely to our own resources in doing the work of God, but we can always depend on the help of the Spirit as we try to do what God wills.

2. *He is our personal companion.* "And I will pray the Father, and he will give you another Counselor, to be with you forever. . . . I will not leave you desolate; I will come to you" (John 14:16-18). He has now come to us in the form of the Spirit, who represents Jesus in our hearts. No Christian need ever feel totally alone, because he or she cannot be. The Spirit will be with us forever as our personal companion for

all of life. What a blessing this is to us when others are not with us. This is a special blessing to the elderly, whose companions have died, and who have no children nearby. Even then, they are not deserted or desolate; for the Spirit is with them day and night. It is just as great a blessing to anyone who is in trouble. So many of our problems cannot be adequately discussed with anyone else. So many of our most important decisions have to be made without the feeling that anyone else really understands. We have to make them on our own. Yet we are not wholly on our own. The Spirit is always present to guide us, encourage us, and help us.

3. *He is our personal teacher.* "But the Counselor, the Holy Spirit, whom the Father will send in my name, he will teach you all things, and bring to your remembrance all that I have said to you" (John 14:26). One of the problems with many schools is that they do not have enough teachers for the number of students. Even in small classes, the teacher cannot spend all the time with any one student, so the student may have to puzzle out for herself or himself what a teacher could quickly make clear. Now there is value in figuring something out for oneself, but some things must be explained or we can never understand them. So it is wonderful to know that the Spirit can be a personal teacher for each of us. He never leaves us completely on our own. He knows the trouble we are having and knows exactly when the time is right for him to teach us something more, and he knows how to let us think things through for ourselves. He is the perfect personal teacher.

4. *He is our personal co-witness.* "But when the Counselor comes, whom I shall send to you from the Father, even the Spirit of truth, who proceeds from the Father, he will bear witness to me; and you also are witnesses" (John 15:26-27). When we witness to others about the life, death, and resurrection of Jesus Christ, the Holy Spirit witnesses along with us. When we tell others that they, too, can be saved by the power of God in Christ Jesus, the Holy Spirit witnesses also. He does this in two ways: He helps us present our testimony,

or preach our sermon, or make our exhortation. He also witnesses to the heart of the person to whom we are speaking.

There is no one to whom we can speak of Christ, to whom the Spirit has not been speaking already. No matter where we go in the world, we can know for sure that the Spirit has been working in hearts there before our arrival. The Holy Spirit is in the world to convince the world of sin, of righteousness, and of judgment (John 16:7-8), and we can be sure that he is always doing his work. He works with all human beings, whether they have heard of God and Christ Jesus or not. With ignorant pagans, whether in this country or in some foreign land, he may not be able to do much except the preliminary work of persuading that person of the reality of sin, the sinfulness of sin, and the reality of righteousness; yet even that is preparation for the gospel.

This is an encouragement to us as we work for God. As we witness to others of the power of God to save from sin, we know that the efficacy of our witness does not depend on us alone. We can do our best and leave the results to God. If the person does not immediately accept Christ and salvation, we know that the Spirit will go on working in the heart and may yet bring that person to salvation. We are not alone in our work for God. The Holy Spirit can work before us and after us. We can speak to the ears of a sinner, but the Spirit works in the deepest thoughts and emotions of the same person. He alone can bring about results.

5. *He is personal convictor.* After we bear witness to one of the power and salvation of God, the work of the Spirit in convincing that person of the truth of your witness goes on in the heart of the hearer. "And when he comes, he will convince the world concerning sin and righteousness and judgment" (John 16:8). We can do our best and must, but the Holy Spirit does the real work. Nothing we do for God can be effective without his blessing and ministry. No preacher can be what God chooses unless the Spirit works in and through the preaching. No sermon is truly effective without the anointing of the Holy Spirit. Neither is any church school class, testimony, song, or anything else done

for God. But with the blessing and anointing of the Spirit, we can do all that God wants us to do.

6. *He is our personal guide.* "When the Spirit of truth comes, he will guide you into all the truth" (John 16:13). In my younger days, I used to hear some of the adults argue on the basis of this text that "we have all the truth there ever could be!" But even then I realized there was something wrong with such an idea. If we already knew all that could be known, we would no longer need the Spirit to guide us into truth. And as long as we are being guided, we have not yet attained to all truth. So we know that we will never know it all, either in this life or in the life to come. God will always know more than we do and will always have more to teach us even in heaven.

Even though we have the guidance of the Spirit all the time, we must never imagine that we are beyond the possibility of being mistaken. The hardest person to teach is the one who thinks he or she already knows. If we are to be guided by the Spirit, we must admit we do not know the way ourselves. Then he will be able to guide us, step by step, into more truth.

The Spirit as Sanctifier

The Holy Spirit is no more holy than the Father and the Son, but he is called holy because he is the one who makes us holy. He is the agent of sanctification. There is much that we do not know about the Divine Trinity, because the Bible does not tell us. We do not know why the three persons each have their separate work to do, but we do know that this is true. Christ became our Savior by dying for us on the cross. While he was in the world, he was teacher, companion, and helper. But now that he is no longer physically in the world, he has given that work over to the Holy Spirit. We have outlined briefly above the way in which he described to the disciples the work that would be given over to the abiding Holy Spirit, whom Christ sent into the world to be another helper like himself.

Clearly the New Testament teaches that the Holy Spirit

convicts us of sin and applies the redemption of Christ to our hearts and lives, so that every Christian has known the work of the Spirit. "Any one who does not have the Spirit of Christ does not belong to him" (Rom. 8:9). If we have not in any sense yielded to the work of the Holy Spirit, then we cannot be Christians. The Holy Spirit first works with us, beginning very early in life, to convince us of the sinfulness of sin and the rightness of obedience. If we refuse to follow the Spirit in this guidance and instruction, he can never lead us to a saving knowledge of Christ, and we will be lost. But if we do follow the Spirit, he will lead us to Christ, and we can be saved. Thus every Christian has already been following the Holy Spirit, even before salvation. It is in this sense that Paul can say that every Christian has the Spirit of Christ.

The Power of the Spirit

The Holy Spirit had a part in the creation of the world, for Genesis 1:2 tells us, "The earth was without form and void, and darkness was upon the face of the deep; and the Spirit of God was moving over the face of the waters." The result of the Spirit's work was that order was brought out of the unformed earth. The Holy Spirit brought forth system, beauty, and order. This has always been the work of the Spirit. Wherever the Spirit of God is given control, there is beauty, purity, and holiness. Always the Holy Spirit demonstrates the power of God. This is power to change things and make them what they ought to be.

The Holy Spirit has power to change people and to make all people what God wills for them to be. But the problem is that people do not often enough surrender to the power of the Holy Spirit and let him make them what they ought to be. So the first work of the Spirit with people is to show them the will of God and seek to persuade them to yield to him.

God's Spirit has fought evil by revealing God's will to the prophets of the Old Testament. He spoke to Amos, Hosea, Joel, Isaiah, Jeremiah, Ezekiel, and all the rest. Through them he revealed his will to humankind. He told them what he wanted to do, what was right, and what was evil. He pointed out the straight and narrow way that leads to life and exhorted them to walk in it and lead others in the straight path.

God gave the prophets the power of the Spirit to strengthen them for their work. In the power of the Spirit they were bold as lions. Nathan stood before the great King David, described his sin, and said, "Thou art the man!" Elijah stood before spineless King Ahab and wicked Queen Jezebel and told them of their sins in no uncertain tones. Amos stood in the midst of the self-righteous, self-satisfied, proud, wicked congregation at Bethel, and said, "Thus says the LORD."

The Spirit of the living God was with the prophets. They preached in the power of the Spirit, and they changed the course of human history.

The supreme example of preaching in the power of the Spirit is found in Jesus Christ. "And Jesus returned in the power of the Spirit into Galilee, and a report concerning him went out through all the surrounding country" (Luke 4:14). In Acts 10:38 Peter said that "God anointed Jesus of Nazareth with the Holy Spirit and with power; how he went about doing good and healing all that were oppressed by the devil, for God was with him." His words carried the unmistakable note of authority and power. His healings involved the going forth of power. His victory over sin was won by the divine power of the Spirit.

The Spirit of Holiness

In the New Testament, the Holy Spirit is referred to more than 250 times. At least twenty-five adjectives or nouns are used in combination with the word *spirit* to describe him, such as "of truth," "of love," "of power," and "holy." But the most common expression is "Holy Spirit." Once he is called the "Spirit of Holiness" (Rom. 1:4). This is equivalent to the term *Holy Spirit* but is a stronger way of emphasizing the holiness of the Spirit and his role in making persons holy. He is called holy to show that he is God, just as the Father and Son are God. But the primary reason for calling him the Holy Spirit is that he is the member of the Trinity who sanctifies Christians. He makes them holy. He is the sanctifier.

So the Holy Spirit is called holy because he is the One who makes holy, not because he is more holy than the other members of the Trinity. We cannot understand why the members of the Godhead, the Triune God, each seem to have their own work to do, since God has not revealed this to us. The whole idea of the Trinity is a mystery too great for our finite minds. But we can easily understand why God has not sought to reveal to us all the mysteries of his own nature. Our minds are simply not capable of understanding God in his full nature. We cannot understand our own natures and are constantly learning new things about human bodies, minds, and emotions. We cannot fully comprehend anything on this earth. How could we possibly understand the whole nature of the God who made the universe? God knew it was impossible and did not seek to tell us the answers to all we could ask. He told us what is necessary for our eternal salvation. The mystery of the Trinity is one of those truths about which we can raise tantalizing questions, but those questions do not have to be answered for us to know and love God. What we do learn from the Bible is that the Holy Spirit is now the administrator of the whole plan of salvation purchased by the blood of Christ according to the will of the Father. Whatever one member of the Trinity does is done with the full concurrence of the other two.

Thus, we can think of the Holy Spirit as the sanctifier. He imparts to us the holiness that enables us to please God. Next we will consider what is meant by the term *entire sanctification.*

Chapter 10:
A Second Crisis

The experience of conversion is a wonderful experience of the grace of God in the heart. The person has, by the grace of God, forsaken sin, accepted God's forgiveness for past sins, and has by faith found an assurance of God's love and power. This is such a turning point in the life of the individual that Jesus called it being "born again." But this term *born again* has in recent years been made totally meaningless by those who apply it to any and every great emotional high.

The New Testament uses a variety of terms for this first great crisis by which one becomes a Christian: *salvation, conversion, redemption, ransom, forgiveness, justification, reconciliation, regeneration, new birth,* and *adoption.* These words are not ten separate actions or experiences, but ten ways of looking at or describing the work of salvation from sin. Human languages are human inventions and are based on human experiences. No words in any human languages can express all that God does when he saves a soul. So we have to use a variety of words, each of which expresses some aspect of the work of God in the human soul.

The First Crisis

By calling conversion the first crisis in Christian experience, we are describing the event as a spiritual crisis. One may have other kinds of crises all through life, but this is a spiritual crisis in which one comes to belong to God to be holy. We call it the first to distinguish it from the second, which is entire sanctification. Sometimes we call these the "two works of grace." We do not at all mean that these are the only two things done for us by the grace of God, but these two are on a different level from the other many works of God on our behalf. God may heal us of our physical afflictions and supply our physical, mental, and financial needs in a multitude of glorious ways, but no matter what else he may do for us, nothing compares with these two works of grace by which he makes us his own people.

Look at some of the wonderful changes wrought in a person at the moment of conversion. Past sins are forgiven by the grace of God (1 John 1:9). The believer in Christ is no longer bound by her or his fleshly weakness to sin but has set the mind on higher things, the things of the Spirit (Rom. 8:1-17). There is no longer the weight of condemnation of sin (Rom. 8:1). The law of the spirit of life in Christ Jesus has broken the power of sin and death (Rom. 8:2). As a result, the Christian does not any longer live in sin (Rom. 6:8; 1 Cor. 15:34). The Christian is being protected by the Spirit from evil (Rom. 8:31-39) and is being led by the Spirit into more Christlike living (Rom. 8:18-27; 2 Cor. 3:18). The whole life and way of living has been changed by the grace of God, and the Christian knows the love of God and loves God in return (1 John 4:19). All this and much more result from the transformation that we call conversion, or salvation.

The crisis that brings all this about is precipitated by the convicting power of the Holy Spirit. The first work of the Holy Spirit in the sinner is to convict the sinner of sin, and of the possibility and necessity of righteousness. The Holy Spirit continues this convicting work until the sinner either accepts the salvation offered by God or dies. (It is possible for the sinner to reject the Spirit so completely and finally that the Spirit will withdraw, but this is not common. Such a person would no longer care about God or goodness and would no longer feel any desire to turn to God, because that desire is a result of the Spirit's work in the heart. So if anyone says, I want to be saved but cannot because I have committed the unpardonable sin against the Spirit, that is clearly not true of this person. If it were, the person would no longer want to be saved.)

So when one is converted in what we call this first crisis experience with God, it is the result of the work of the Spirit in bringing the person to that point. The work of conversion, which cannot be brought about by human power, is done by the Spirit. We are saved by the blood of Christ, but the power is applied to our hearts by the Holy Spirit. All this is done by the grace of God, by the unmerited favor of God, so we call this a work of grace.

This first work of grace is often called "initial sanctification." This is not a bad term since conversion initiates the process of sanctification, which is continued in growth in grace and is brought to a completion in the second work of grace, entire sanctification, after which the spiritual growth can continue with less hindrance.

The primary meaning of holiness or sanctification, we can remember, is belonging to God. The sinner does not really belong to God, though he or she was created by God and is totally answerable to God for all he or she does. But every Christian belongs to God and has been purchased by the blood of Jesus Christ. The Christian has forsaken sin, been forgiven, and has accepted by faith the salvation made possible by the death and resurrection of Christ. The Christian can thus be called holy. Yet this holiness is not complete and must be considered initial, or preliminary.

All Christians are called holy in the New Testament, in spite of the fact that they sometimes had much to learn about living for God and many changes yet to be made in their lives. For this reason some have called this "positional holiness." Just as Old Testament sacrifices were sanctified by being on the altar, so New Testament Christians are made holy by their position at the cross of Christ. The Christian may have much to learn about the ethical implications of conversion but cannot continue doing what he or she knows is sinful.

The Christian does not continue living in sin, for she or he has died to sin (Rom. 6:12). The new convert does not know all about what God requires and may therefore make many blunders. She or he may continue doing things that grieve the heart of God but cannot do what is known to be displeasing to God. So the Christian does not go on sinning but is required to be holy in every intention of the heart and will.

Growing Sanctification

George Allen Turner uses the term *positional sanctification* for conversion and calls this growing sanctification "actual sanctification."[1] I like to call it "growing sanctification," or "growth in grace." The new Christian begins immediately to grow in grace and in understanding the requirements of God both ethically and spiritually. So much intellectual, ethical, and spiritual growth begins to take place. Just as the newborn infant must begin to grow physically and intellectually, so the newborn Christian must grow or die.

That this spiritual growth is necessary in the Christian is universally affirmed. Peter strongly exhorts us to strive for this growth in specific areas (2 Pet. 1:5-11). All Christians know that we must continue to grow or die. But this universal agreement breaks down when we suggest that this process of growth in holiness can come to some point of completion in love before death. But this is just what is meant by entire sanctification.

Entire Sanctification

Entire sanctification refers to the completed process by which the Holy Spirit makes his home in the human soul. It does not mean that the process of spiritual growth has been completed, for growth is speeded up at this point. Rather, it means that the person is wholly committed to God, and that the Holy Spirit has accepted the invitation to dwell in the soul and to do all he comes to do.

The term *entire sanctification* comes from Paul's statement in 1 Thessalonians 5:23: "May the God of peace himself sanctify you wholly; and may your spirit and soul and body be kept sound and blameless at the coming of our Lord Jesus

Christ." This expresses the idea of the completeness of the holiness the Christian experiences after the "second work of grace" by the Holy Spirit.

Wilber Dayton ably explains the nature of entire sanctification in this way:

> The primary idea of holiness has to do with relationship to God. The temple was holy because it was God's house. The furnishings of the temple were holy in that they were separated from other uses and were dedicated to the service of God. The priests, likewise, were separated from relationships and activities that would pervert or mar their special calling. The primary idea of holiness was not in what they were separated from, but to whom they were dedicated. Their separation was not an end in itself, as in pagan asceticism. It found its meaning in dedication to God. . . . Consequently, entire sanctification has to do with the completeness and perfection of that relationship with God.[2]

Note how Dr. Dayton builds on the concept of holiness that we have already considered in previous chapters. Holiness is not merely separation from sin and the world, but on the other hand it is separation to God. It is a personal relationship with God, that the person chooses voluntarily in response to God's gracious, loving call to come to him. So every Christian is holy, but that holiness can, by the grace of God and the work of the Holy Spirit, come to a point of completion that is a long step beyond initial, or positional sanctification.

The completeness of sanctification has to do with the completeness of our relationship with God. It does not mean one is then absolutely or infinitely perfect, as some have accused us of believing. It is the relationship that is perfect, a relationship of perfect love. God loves us, and we have come to love God in return. This love had its beginning in conversion but could not come to completion until we had presented our saved selves to God in unconditional surrender and commitment. Then the Holy Spirit could complete the work of sanctification and seal in us a depth of relationship with God that we were not able to know before.

Much of the discussion of entire sanctification has centered on the cleansing that takes place at that time, in the attempt to decide just how to describe what is cleansed out of the heart in order to make the person holy. Much of this effort is wasted. What is cleansed is the heart, soul, mind, and will. The cleanser is the Holy Spirit. We do not have to know exactly what he does or how he does it. All we have to do is to turn ourselves over to him in unconditional, unreserved surrender and let him do for us, to us, and in us exactly what he chooses. We do not have to work out in our minds a perfect theological concept of the work of the Holy Spirit in sanctification. We need only to study carefully the biblical descriptions and references and to seek always to be scriptural in our terminology of holiness and sanctification. Then the Spirit can guide us in our search for the whole truth and, most of all, for the whole and complete will of God in our lives.

The New Testament uses a variety of terms for the experience of entire sanctification and its results: Christian perfection, holiness, perfect love, gift of the Holy Spirit, purification, cleansing, baptism of the Spirit, and fullness of the Spirit. John Wesley taught us that using these terms in scriptural ways is more important than having a finely tuned consistency in our system of theology. We should seek to rid ourselves of nonscriptural terms that can lead all too easily to division and dissension and use New Testament terms in scriptural ways.

As we seek to understand what the New Testament says the sanctified person is like, we note the following conditions or qualities:

1. One has been transformed by the renewing of the mind by the work of the Holy Spirit (Rom. 12:2).

2. One is God's very own possession voluntarily given to him. This means total commitment to the work of the Holy Spirit.

3. One is "filled with the Spirit." This phrase refers to the ease with which the Spirit can work his will in the heart and mind of the person who is totally committed to him. It does

120

not mean that the human personality has been supplanted by the Holy Spirit, but that the person has yielded self so completely to the Spirit that God can freely work with and through the human personality to do what he chooses. The human personality is not suppressed by the Spirit but guided by the Holy Spirit.

4. One is empowered by the Spirit to do the work of God in the world (Acts 1:8).

5. The sanctified one is growing fruits of the Spirit (Rom. 12:9-21; Gal. 5:22-23).

6. He or she is seeking to add Christian virtues as God assists (2 Pet. 1:57).

7. The person has a growing love for God (Rom. 5:5).

Nature of the Second Crisis

Since sanctification comes by grace through faith, it is not something to be achieved. Like salvation, which also comes through faith, it can come in a moment of time as it is given by God. It is not something that can be achieved by human effort or by gradual growth. Those who believe that we grow into it usually believe that we can never come to any point of completion in this life. Many believe that we grow in grace all our lives and that at the moment of death we receive the holiness that will enable us to be with God in heaven. But not a single word of Scripture supports such an idea. Paul speaks of death as an enemy to be finally overcome at the resurrection of all at the second coming of Christ. Death is not our friend, to sanctify us, but an enemy. A defeated enemy, but still an enemy.

Sanctification is spoken of in the New Testament as completed in this life. We do not have to wait until death to finish working it out by our own efforts. When Paul said, "Work out your own salvation," he was not speaking of us working to save or sanctify ourselves. He simply meant that after we are saved, we must work to keep our lives godly, and to live lives worthy of the gospel of salvation that we had accepted by faith and by the grace of God. Note the whole passage:

Therefore, my beloved, as you have always obeyed, so now, not only as in my presence but much more in my absence, work out your own salvation with fear and trembling; for God is at work in you, both to will and to work for his good pleasure (Phil. 2:12-13).

Clearly our work is as co-workers with God and not solely our work. Our only hope of succeeding in our work lies in the fact that God is working with us to assist us in doing his will.

The fact that this is a second crisis experience can be seen from the fact that all Christians have the Holy Spirit (Rom. 8:9; 1 Cor. 3:16; 6:19; Eph. 2:2; Gal. 3:12). Yet it is equally clear that less than all are filled with the Spirit (Eph. 3:19; 5:18).

Another line of reasoning is presented by the great Greek scholar H. C. G. Moule:

We gather very plainly that the "Filling" is not identical in idea with the initial work of the Spirit as Life-giver. The filling is always seen as taking place where there is already present the New Birth; and the possession of that Birth is thus the occasion for a holy desire and longing to possess in some sense the filling.[3]

The New Testament accounts clearly show that conversion precedes the infilling of the Holy Spirit. This is true in all the accounts in the Book of Acts. Look at some of the accounts and see how this is true.

1. *The disciples were converted before Pentecost.* It is scarcely necessary to prove this. If they were not converted they were certainly the most godly of all sinners! They believed in Jesus Christ. They trusted in God to help them. They prayed regularly. They had left all the world to follow Jesus. They were the best people in the world at that time. It would be strange indeed if Jesus, who healed the paralyzed man and forgave his sins (Mark 2:5), would not forgive the sins of his disciples! Further, Jesus told his disciples to rejoice "that your names are written in heaven" (Luke 10:20).

2. *The church in Samaria.* Since many of the people of

Samaria were saved under the preaching of Philip, they were converted Christians (Acts 8:5-8). But we are told in verses 14-17 of the same chapter that after they had been converted under the preaching of Philip, Peter and John went to Samaria, preached to them about the Holy Spirit, and prayed for them. As a result they did receive the Holy Spirit. Thus they were converted at one time and filled with the Holy Spirit at a later time.

3. *The household of Cornelius.* We are told in Acts 10:2 that Cornelius was a devout and righteous man. This fact is strongly emphasized. We are also told in Acts 10:44-45 that Peter preached to him and to his household and that the Holy Spirit came to them and filled them. Though some have argued that Cornelius was only on the way to becoming a Jewish proselyte, he was clearly a godly man. It is not too much to say that he also was converted at one time and filled with the Spirit later.

4. *The disciples at Ephesus.* In Acts 18:24-28 we read that Apollos preached at Ephesus and won converts. But we are told in 19:12 that after Paul came to them, preached to them about the Holy Spirit, and prayed for them, they did receive the Holy Spirit. Ephesians 1:13 also makes clear that the disciples in Ephesus were converted at one time and after that were sealed with the Holy Spirit of promise.

5. *The Thessalonian church.* In Acts 17 we read that Paul went to Thessalonica and preached the gospel and that many believed. Paul says more about this in 1 Thessalonians 3:12. Later in that same letter to the Thessalonian church, Paul stated that he was praying that God would sanctify them wholly (5:23-24).

These examples are not full proof that being filled with the Holy Spirit always comes after conversion. One could argue that this was true only for the first converts in the very early days of the gospel age and that it can be different now. But when coupled with the other reasons and with the experience of most Christians, these are strong support for the concept of a second crisis. Not a single text describes conversion and the baptism of the Holy Spirit as occurring at the same time.

On the other hand, the New Testament does not support three works of grace, such as conversion, sanctification, and the filling with the Spirit, or the idea of conversion, filling of the Spirit, and baptism of the Spirit. The latter two phrases, "filling with the Spirit" and "baptism with the Spirit," are used synonymously and about the same number of times in the Book of Acts.

Why Two Works of Grace?

All Christians believe that conversion and holiness are necessary if one is to go to heaven. But all Christians do not agree on how this takes place. The major disagreement is on the time when one becomes holy enough to get to heaven. As we have seen, some believe that this final sanctification becomes complete only at the moment of death. Others believe that we get the whole, complete experience of sanctification at the moment of conversion. The latter say that God never does anything by halves. What God does in and for a person, he does all at once and never in piecemeal fashion. So they insist that God does not save a person at one time and sanctify her or him wholly at a later time.

This reasoning will not stand in the light of the Scripture. God created the world, but he did it in six stages, as Genesis 1 describes clearly. When God led the Israelites out of Egypt he did not transport them immediately to the Promised Land but led them first to Mount Sinai where they spent a year and a half, then to Kadesh-Barnea for forty years, and finally to the Promised Land. When Jesus healed the blind man of Bethsaida, the man could not see clearly at first but saw men "look like trees, walking." Then Jesus laid his hands on the man's eyes again, and this time the man could see clearly (Mark 8:22-26). God does things in his way, for his own good reasons, that he does not have to explain to us. If God chooses to do things in a way that looks less than perfect to us, we need to understand that we have no right to judge his ways. We must simply do our best to fit into his plans unquestioningly. Yet we can understand something of the reasons why God saves us and then sanctifies us entirely.

One of the first important facts to note in the study of entire sanctification is that the words relating to it are the words of sacrifice. Pope underlines this fact in regard to the whole process by which a human being is made acceptable to God:

> The terms which belong to this branch of Christian theology . . . constitute the largest class of homogeneous phrases in the New Testament. . . . They embrace the entire vocabulary of the Altar, its sacrifices, oblation and priesthood, divine and human; sanctification, dedication, presentation, hallowing, consecration; sprinkling, washing, and putting away sin; purity, sanctity, love, and holiness.[4]

We can see the importance of this fact as we examine closely an important passage: Romans 12:1-2.

> I appeal to you therefore, brethren, by the mercies of God, to present your bodies as a living sacrifice, holy and acceptable to God, which is your spiritual worship. Do not be conformed to this world but be transformed by the renewal of your mind, that you may prove what is the will of God, what is good and acceptable and perfect.

Note first that the Apostle is here using the language of sacrifice, as typically used in the Old Testament worship in the tabernacle and temple. The word *present* is the term used in the Old Testament for bringing a sacrifice to God at the altar and offering it to God.

1. *This exhortation is addressed to those who were Christians.* That they were already converted is clearly shown by the fact that the sacrifice they were to present to God is to be living, holy, and well-pleasing to God. Furthermore, this sacrifice is not some animal from the field or food from the kitchen, but their own bodies. Of course, Paul is not speaking only of the physical body, but of the whole person. He did not speak of the heart, soul, or mind, for then some would have been all the quicker to feel that their heart was God's, while using

their bodies for sin. So he used the term *body* to represent the whole personality, the whole person. We must give our own whole selves to God, then he will have all of us, body, mind, heart, soul, will, and all our possessions.

The body that is presented to God as a sacrifice is to meet three tests. It must be holy, living, and well-pleasing to God. In the same way, the Old Testament sacrifice of a lamb had to meet three tests, as we can see from a study of Leviticus. First, it had to be a lamb that was alive, not dead. The farmer could not bring to God a lamb that had died of exposure during the night, for the lamb offered to God had to be alive. Second, it had to be a lamb, for that was "well-pleasing to God." It could not be a pig wrapped in lambskin, or any unclean animal. It had to be the right kind of animal for a sacrifice, or God would reject both it and the person who sought to offer it. Third, it had to be holy. For the animal sacrifice, this meant that the animal must be whole and not sick or deformed. This does not at all mean that God does not accept sick or deformed persons; the animal's perfection was only a symbol of the spiritual holiness that we must have if we are to present ourselves to God.

Now if we consider these three conditions for an acceptable sacrifice and think of their spiritual meaning, we can see what God requires of us. To present ourselves to God, we must be alive spiritually. That is, we must not be "dead through . . . trespasses and sins" (Eph. 2:1), but "alive together with Christ" (v. 5). This clearly means that we must have been converted and must be still living in Christ. To be "well-pleasing to God," we must be the right kind of person—Christian, Christlike. To be holy is to have the sins washed away, forgiven, and to be living now so we are acceptable to God. All of this means that the sinner is not capable of presenting herself or himself to God in obedience to this verse.

2. *An appeal to the mercies of God would mean little to those who had not already been saved by the grace of God.* Paul was not speaking here to sinners in need of forgiveness and conversion, but to born again Christians who already loved God and were serving him.

3. *Since the sacrifice had to be holy, the person already had experienced "initial sanctification" at conversion.* Paul is then speaking of a second work of the grace of God in the heart of one who already knows God.

4. *The only sacrifice that is acceptable to God is one that is free from slavery to any other master.* One who is living for the devil and is in bondage to sin cannot give herself or himself to God as here commanded. Yet Jesus said very plainly, "Truly, truly, I say to you, everyone who commits sin is a slave to sin" (John 8:34). So no sinner is fit to be given to God as a sacrifice.

A most important point in the Old Testament is the idea of *cherem*. This Hebrew word is nearly impossible to translate consistently into English with one word. It represents an idea that is foreign to our way of thinking and has to be translated by a variety of words as it is used in different contexts. It is often rendered "devoted" but sometimes "utterly destroyed." To understand why, it is instructive to look at the conquest of Jericho, as described in Joshua 6.

Chapter 11:
Entire Sanctification

Entire Sanctification is the term that we are using for the "Second work of grace in the heart." As we have seen, the term comes from Paul's expression in 1 Thessalonians 5:23, "May the God of peace himself sanctify you wholly." It is called *entire* because the whole person is holy, or sanctified. This work of sanctification is done by the Holy Spirit and is possible because of the saved person completely dedicating his or her whole saved self to God. It is not that the person has no more to learn and no more progress to make, but that the person has, through the unreserved commitment of the whole self to God, made the total personality available to the cleansing, empowering, enabling work of the Holy Spirit. The Spirit has then done his work on the whole person—body, mind, soul, spirit, intellect, emotions, will, and all. The person belongs wholly to God.

This whole idea is so simple that anyone can grasp it. Yet it has been so complicated by the discussions that have raged over it that there is much confusion. Some of the confusion centers on false expectations of what the sanctified person should be like. So we need to consider some of the things entire sanctification does not do.

What Sanctification Does Not Do

1. *Entire sanctification does not end temptation.* One of the reasons people have trouble with the idea of sanctification is

that they do all they are told to do and yet do not feel that they are sanctified. They do not feel that the Holy Spirit has done the work in their hearts. They feel this way because they expect certain things to happen that do not happen. When their high expectations are disappointed, they feel that nothing at all has happened. Thus they are discouraged and may decide either that there is nothing to the idea of entire sanctification or that it is not for them.

When such a person prays for the Holy Spirit to sanctify his or her heart, that one may believe for a little while that the work has been done. But then comes a strong temptation, and the Christian feels that surely such a strong temptation could not come to one who is sanctified and wonders what is wrong.

We all need to understand that temptations will come to us as long as we are in this world. This temporal world is a place of testing and probation. Probation, when used in this theological sense, means that we are here to prove ourselves true to God and to ourselves. Temptations are both tests of our love for God and one of the means by which we grow stronger and draw closer to God. Perhaps it is truer to say that the temptation is not itself a means of grace, but that the overcoming of temptation by the grace of God makes us stronger spiritually.

Yield not to temptation, for yielding is sin.
Each victory will help you some other to win.

When we remember that Jesus was sorely tempted (Heb. 2:18; 4:15), we can more easily face the fact that we will never outgrow temptation or come to any high state of spirituality that will place us beyond temptation. So the fact that a person is tempted does not have anything to do with the reality of one's sanctification.

2. *Sanctification does not make sin impossible.* This follows from the fact that one can still be tempted. It needs to be emphasized; it will always be possible for the very best and most mature Christian to commit sin, if he or she so chooses, or if he or she allows himself or herself to drift away from a close personal relationship with God.

130

While God does not make sinning impossible for the sanctified Christian, he does, by his grace, make it possible not to sin. "Not impossible to sin, but possible not to sin!" That is the classic way of putting the matter. God himself provides the power to overcome temptation without sinning (1 Cor. 10:12-13). But the individual Christian must use this power to struggle successfully against sin and temptation.

3. *Sanctification does not make us infallible.* We will continue to make mistakes as long as we live in this world. We make mistakes in judgment, mistakes in knowledge, and we fail at times to do as well as we know to do because of frailty, tiredness, and plain human weakness. Yet we need not sin. We can have perfect love for God and not be able to show that love in a perfect manner. We can have perfect love for others and fail to make that love known to others at all times. We may fail in this way because of lack of perfect knowledge or our failure to understand how the other person perceives our actions. So we will never progress to the point that others will see us as being perfect, even though we may be perfect in the eyes of God. This is true because God has perfect knowledge of our abilities and lack of them. He knows how much he can expect of each of us at our present state of growth, experience, and understanding. He never expects too much, or too little. He knows whether we love him or not and how well. He is the perfect judge and the perfect helper. He loves us with an unchanging, undying love and is always ready and eager to help us do better. Even if we turn away from him, he is eager to bring us back to repentance and to full fellowship with him. All of this makes loving and serving him all our days a joyous adventure.

4. *Sanctification does make growing and learning necessary for us.* In order to go on pleasing God, we must continue to grow in grace (2 Pet. 3:18). We cannot simply stay the same and still please God. Even though he is pleased with our state of maturity and progress at one moment, he knows that we must continue in our power to grow or we will fall.

We grow by making use of the means of grace that God has supplied to us. We must feed on the Word of God regularly. It is God's message to us. It will help us to grow as we go on studying it, meditating on it, and praying for guidance in understanding it. The Bible is not a book we can pick up for the first time and immediately understand. But neither is it so difficult that we average Christians can never know what it is all about. None of us will ever understand everything in the Bible, at least in this life. But all of us can understand enough to gain from it strength and grace to live our lives so as to keep on pleasing God.

To grow spiritually, we must also learn to love regular prayer. This is something one must cultivate through discipline. We need to pray regularly, just as we need to read the Bible daily. To build up this habit of daily prayer, we must remind ourselves to pray daily at the most regular times we can manage, whether we feel like it or not. In this way it becomes a life-long habit and will not fail to keep us when the going is rough.

To grow, we must cultivate the love of Christian fellowship. We do this by taking advantage of every opportunity to be with God's people, both in and out of the church services. A Christian who really wants to grow will never miss a service of worship. She or he will seek to pray earnestly for the spiritual blessings God wants to give us in such services. As we pray for those who do not always please us, we will come to love them more and more. If God can love them— and he does—then we can love them by his grace.

Finally, to grow in the Lord, we must resist every temptation and pray for constant victory in every time of trouble. Giving in or giving up will bring the whole venture to a halt. It is through determined resistance to evil that we are enabled to grow more and more. We still have to work at our resistance to evil and seek to add to our love for God. God will give us the victory only if we do the best we can and then leave the rest to him.

What Sanctification Does

As we have looked at some of the things entire sanctification does not do, we must not get the impression that it is not much of an experience. It is a tremendous change for every Christian, and it changes the whole life for the better.

1. *The Holy Spirit begins dwelling in the heart (John 14:17).*
"You know him, for he dwells with you, and will be in you."
Verse 23 expresses it even more interestingly: "If a man loves
me, he will keep my word, and my Father will love him, and
we will come to him and make our home with him." As one
preacher put it, "The Father, Son and Holy Spirit will set up
housekeeping in your soul." This is not far from the literal
meaning of the Greek of this verse.

The complete dedication of the saved self to God allows
the Holy Spirit to move in and take control of the life in a
new and more positive way. Until that commitment is made,
he cannot do all that he desires in the person's heart and life
because of the remaining resistance that the devil can cultivate. But when the Christian gives up the total self to the
control of God, the Spirit is able to do more in and through
and for the Christian than ever before. This is the first great
result of the experience of sanctification.

2. *The Holy Spirit gives power.* Shortly before the Day of
Pentecost, Jesus spoke earnestly with his disciples about their
future without his physical presence. Just before his ascen-
sion, he said to them, "But you shall receive power when the
Holy Spirit has come upon you; and you shall be my
witnesses in Jerusalem and in all Judea and Samaria and to
the end of the earth" (Acts 1:8).

The power of which Jesus spoke is first power to stand.
Notice the number of times in the next few chapters that the
boldness and courage of the disciples are mentioned. They
had courage to stand against all their opponents, which they
had not had before the coming of the Holy Spirit upon them.
They were not any longer afraid to do the right thing in spite
of opposition. On the day of the Crucifixion, they had
"followed afar off," but now they wanted everybody to
know just where they stood. They had strength now to resist
temptations to which they had before been sorely inclined to
yield.

This power was necessary, for they no longer had the
support of the physical presence of Jesus to help them and to
encourage them. So God had given them "another Counse-

lor"—the Holy Spirit —just as Christ had promised them. They were not alone but had the abiding presence of the Holy Spirit to do for them constantly what Christ had done for them for three years.

Note carefully that this power is not some impersonal quality that they were given once for all. It is rather the abiding presence of the Holy Spirit, who works in and through the Christian, "both to will and to work for his good pleasure" (Phil. 2:13). He himself chooses what we should do and enables us to do it. We are not simply given power that we can control and use to do as we please. We cannot control the Holy Spirit, he seeks to control us, by guiding us through our own minds, knowledge, understanding, and will, to do what he wants done. He does not answer our commands, since it is his prerogative to command us. The arrogant ignoring of this point leads to all sorts of distortions of the Christian life and work.

On the other hand, the Holy Spirit does not take over our minds and wills, to make us do his will whether we want to or not. As an old song used to put it: "He doesn't compel us to go, Oh no, he just makes us willing to go." Yet he does not force us to be willing to do the right thing, for God will never overrule the human will. He created it for a purpose. As long as we are in this life, we are free to do right or wrong. So the Holy Spirit does not take control of our lives in that sense. He does in us through us, and for us only what we allow.

This fact is the reason why total submission and unreserved dedication are essential if the Holy Spirit is to sanctify us wholly and begin his abiding in us. He does much in us of which we are not aware and works through us in ways we do not understand or appreciate; yet he never violates our own personal wills. We can grieve him if we choose to reject him at any time. We can drive him away or drift away from his presence, so that he may eventually leave us to our own devices and destruction. But as long as we remain totally committed to him and his will, he will continue to work in and through us for our good, for the salvation of others, and for the glory of God. He gives all the power we need. But it is power to do God's will, not ours.

Jesus said that the power the disciples would receive was power to be his witnesses. It is power to live a life that will support what is said about the gospel and it is power to preach and teach the gospel in such a way that we reach the hearts of those who need it. So all the abilities and gifts that the Holy Spirit bestows are not for the sake of the person who receives them but are to give her or him the ability to do the work of the gospel. Paul makes this clear:

> And his gifts were that some should be apostles, some prophets, some evangelists, some pastors and teachers, to equip the saints for the work of ministry, for building up the body of Christ (Eph. 4:11-12).

The King James Version and the first edition of the Revised Standard Version both placed a comma after the word *saints*, giving a false impression of Paul's meaning. The second edition of RSV properly omitted the comma; the Greek wording clearly states that the purpose of equipping the saints was so they might do the work of the ministry. This is the purpose of the power given by the Holy Spirit.

3. *The Spirit leads us into all truth.* He does this, not by making us suddenly educated, but by leading us step by step into all the truth we need to know. Like any good teacher, he teaches us in carefully planned progressive stages as we are able to master them.

When I was a boy, I used to hear some people argue on the basis of this text that those who are sanctified "have all the truth" and do not need to learn anything. I soon decided that those who were arguing in this way did not know everything! I could see that their own reasoning was poor, their exegesis was faulty, and that they apparently did not understand the English grammar of this plain scripture. Most important, they did not comprehend the vastness of their own lack of understanding. The truth is that none of us knows very much in this world, in comparison with all there is for us to know. I am convinced that even in heaven we will understand or comprehend everything. Even there we will go on learning all through eternity. We will never attain to the omniscience of God, so we will never know all things. We will know him more completely and more intimately, and that is enough.

4. *The Holy Spirit binds us together in real unity.* This is the way God builds the church. We are a part of the church as soon as we are converted, but we are built into it more firmly as the Holy Spirit works in us more freely and binds us together with other Christians in a growing love-bond that is stronger than any other bond on earth.

Jesus prayed for this in his great high-priestly prayer for the disciples on the night before he was crucified:

> They are not of the world, even as I am not of the world. Sanctify them in the truth; thy word is truth. . . . I do not pray for these only, but also for those who believe in me through their word, that they may all be one; even as thou, Father, art in me, and I in thee, that they also may be in us, so that the world may believe that thou has sent me (John 17:16-17, 20-21).

Notice the close association of sanctification and unity in this passage. We also see here that the kind of unity that Jesus prayed for is the unity of the three persons of the Trinity. He prayed that we might be one in this same deep unity.

To be one in this sense is far more than simply attending the same church or having the same name over the door of the building. It means that we should be bound together in the close bond of divine love for one another. If we truly love one another in this way, we will overlook one another's faults in order to see the good in each other. We will seek constantly to forgive one another and work together in close harmony to do the work of God. We will understand that doing the work of God is far more important than having our own way, getting more credit for what is done than others, or even getting as much honor as we deserve. Most of us have difficulty in our own strength to be always what we ought to be in the church. We must have the empowering, cleansing, enabling love of God, as poured into our hearts by the Holy Spirit. This is what makes possible the real oneness of God's people, the Church.

5. *The Holy Spirit fills with the love of God.* Probably the most important passage in the whole New Testament regarding the work of the Holy Spirit is one that is not usually emphasized. In Romans 5:5 Paul wrote, "Hope does not disappoint us, because God's love has been poured into our hearts through the Holy Spirit which has been given to us." We talk too much about some of the more spectacular things the Holy Spirit does for us, and too little about the work of pouring into us the love God has for us, the love we ought to have for God, the love we must have for other Christians, and the godly love for sinners that drives us to win others to Christ.

When Jesus was asked by a scribe which was the greatest of all the commandments in the Law, he replied,

The first is, "Hear, O Israel: The Lord our God, the Lord is one; and you shall love the Lord your God with all your heart, and with all your soul, and with all your mind, and with all your strength." The second is this, "You shall love your neighbor as yourself" Deuteronomy 6:4, 5.

Godly love, then, is the most important gift God can give us through the Holy Spirit. This is why John Wesley was correct when he constantly stressed the importance of understanding holiness as being perfect love.

You should be thoroughly sensible of this, "the heaven of heavens is love." There is nothing higher in religion; there is in effect, nothing else; if you look for anything but more love, you are looking wide of the mark, you are getting out of the royal way.[1]

The very essence of holiness is love. Love for God truly leaves no room for sin. The heart that is filled with the love of God cannot have sin in it. This is not to say that that person cannot possibly sin, but that to sin requires that the love of God be let to leak out of the heart first, then sin is possible. Or temptation can be such that it turns the attention away from God, and then one can sin. But no one can sin while gazing in love upon one's Lord. Sin and godly love are direct opposites. They can no more dwell in the same heart at the same time than light and darkness can be in the same place at the same time. Even the light of a tiny candle drives away all the darkness within reach. Wherever the light of the candle is, darkness is not. But do not try to measure the light of your candle; just make sure it is lit!

This love of God can only be poured into your heart through the Holy Spirit. It cannot be worked up by yourself. It is the very nature of sin to kill the love of God. One may feel something of an emotion and put the word love to it, but the godly love that the Spirit gives is far different from anything else that may go by the name of love.

Paul pointed out (1 Cor. 13:13) that all the good actions one can do, and all the miracles one could claim to perform, are nothing unless one has godly love. This means that we should not seek for the powers granted by the Spirit unless and until we are sure that we have our hearts filled with godly love. Furthermore, if one's heart is filled with godly love, then one does not truly want anything else. The desire for other gifts is smothered by love for God himself. If then other gifts are granted, they are only for the glory of God and not to satisfy any strong craving of ours. Great gifts are not needed to satisfy us, but only God and his glory. This truly is the point of the whole discussion of spiritual gifts in 1 Corinthians 12, 13, and 14.

How to Be Sanctified

1. *Be sure you are converted and living a clean Christian life.* Only the saved life and person can be given to God in the kind of dedication that makes possible the sanctification by the Holy Spirit. There is no use kidding ourselves about this. God will not accept any sinful sacrifice on the spiritual altar of dedication.

Jesus promised the Spirit to his disciples, to those who had already come to a saving knowledge of God through him. So he said that the world of sinners cannot know the Spirit or receive him into their hearts.

If you love me, you will keep my commandments. And I will pray the Father, and he will give you another Counselor, to be with you forever, even the Spirit of truth, whom the world cannot receive, because it neither sees him nor knows him; you know him, for he dwells with you, and will be in you (John 14:15-17).

There are then two primary reasons why we must be saved first and then entirely sanctified by the Holy Spirit. First, only the saved person can dedicated the self to God acceptably. Second, the sinner cannot truly know the Spirit, who is the sanctifier. So it is wrong to seek for sanctification in order to be sure of personal salvation. One should be sure of salvation and then present that saved self to God as a living, holy, sacrifice, well-pleasing to God (Rom. 12:1).

2. *Dedicate your saved self to God.* This means to give your saved self to God wholly, unreservedly, without any expectation of taking control of yourself again. Put yourself wholly in God's hands and leave yourself there. This commitment of yourself is for life and eternity. As Christ gave himself for us, so we ought to give ourselves totally to him. We recognize that we belong to him and not to ourselves. He bought us with a great price. He is worth more than all the world to us. His love and approval are worth more than the whole universe. It is only our "reasonable service" or our "spiritual worship" to give ourselves to him in this total way (Rom. 12:1).

3. *Die to self and selfishness (Gal. 2:20).* In a very real sense, this death to self and selfishness cannot take place without the work of the Holy Spirit. But we must be most willing for this death to take place. We cannot hold on to our own desires and wishes and expect God to take control of our lives.

What we mean by "dying to self" is that we no longer let our own desires and wishes stand between us and God. We do not stubbornly continue to do what we wish but simply submit to whatever we feel that God would have us do. In

139

other words, we are not to wait for any emotional crisis of "dying," for that may not happen to us at all. Some people go through such a crisis with no doubt in their minds that they have "died to self" and that they have had a great experience with God. With others there is no such great struggle, so they are tempted to feel that they do not have all God has for them, since they experienced no tremendous crisis point. These submitted to God so gently and easily that there was no struggle at all. But the experience of entire sanctification is just as real without such a struggle as with one. The point is that one must be wholly submitted to the will of God. It is not how one gets to this point, but whether or not God can have his way with us.

When we have met the conditions for entire sanctification as well as we know how, then we can simply trust and believe that God has done the work in us that he wants to do. There is no point in comparing our experience with those of others around us. Each person's experience is unique. Neither should we worry constantly that we may not have known all the conditions. If we learn more, then we can immediately do what we now know and continue on our way rejoicing that God is with us.

Chapter 12:
The Spirit in the Church

The Holy Spirit enters into individual Christians and makes his home in them. We have seen some of the ways in which he then helps the Christian live a holy life before God, and we will consider further ways in a later chapter. But just now we need to consider what the Bible says about how the Spirit works in and through the church. Since the church is made up of the individual Christians, the church is not a personality in itself. So the Holy Spirit has to work in the church by working in and through the individual members or Christians. He works in the whole by working in and through the parts. He controls the whole church by leading the individual Christians to think and act as God wishes. If enough of the members are wholly committed to God, then the Spirit can do in the church the work that needs to be done. Individual members may be mistaken at times about the leading of God, and all the members may be mistaken sometimes. But in the long run, God will find a way, through the work and guidance of the Spirit in the individuals, to get done the work which he chooses to do.

The primary point here is simple and clear. God can only work in the church by working in individual members of the church. He speaks to the church by speaking to individual Christians. He guides the church by guiding individuals. He leads sinners to salvation by means of soul-winning Christians. He preaches to the church by speaking to and through a preacher, whether that preacher is the pastor or some Christian to whom God has spoken. He heals the sick through the prayers and faith of Christians. He leads the church to do the right things, and to make good decisions through leading individual Christians to make wise, godly decisions.

Sometimes the Spirit seems to lead all the Christians in a congregation toward a single decision on which they are unanimous. At other times, there is much discussion and puzzling over a matter without any clear guidance. God sometimes lets us search a long time for the right way to build a building or select a pastor. At such times, we must not say that the Spirit is not working. This may be the only way he can make us learn some of the lessons we need to know. At such times, we must seek to be as humble, teachable, and cooperative as God would have us be. If we can do this, God will eventually show us clearly the way to go. I may have to learn through others some of the problems with my way. I may have to give in to the opinions of others for the sake of harmony and unity in the church. I may have to let others have their way even when I am sure my way is better so long as their way is not sinful! I may have to wait for others to change their opinions, or I may have to change mine. But if we will be determined to work together, and to follow God's guidance wherever he may lead, then the Spirit will be able to lead us in good ways.

After all, God has kept the church alive for nearly two thousand years; surely he can guide it safely to the end of time, even if all do not follow my intelligent guidance! Faith in God, patience with one another, and submission to God and to the will of the church is bound to take the church forward under the leadership of the Holy Spirit.

Gift of the Spirit

The gift of the Spirit is the Holy Spirit himself. God has graciously given him to those who meet the conditions. He had promised this gift of the Spirit in the Old Testament

(Ezek. 36:27; 37:14; Joel 2:28-29). John the Baptist and Jesus had both repeated the promise and made it more specific. On the Day of Pentecost the promise was first fulfilled, so that now the gift can be received by any who will meet the conditions. These conditions were described in the previous chapter.

It is all too common for us to be careless of the value of this great gift from God. When we stop to consider what this is all about, we realize that it is amazing and almost beyond belief that the Creator of the whole universe would care enough about these insignificant human beings that he would come to live within us! Solomon felt the force of this thought and expressed it in his prayer at the dedication of the Temple he had built:

> But will God indeed dwell on the earth? Behold, heaven and the highest heaven cannot contain thee; how much less this house which I have built! (1 Kings 8:27).

Yet Isaiah, with his glorious vision of God's plan, declared:

> For thus says the high and lofty One who inhabits eternity, whose name is Holy: 'I dwell in the high and holy place, and also with him who is of a contrite and humble spirit, to revive the spirit of the humble, and to revive the heart of the contrite' (Isa. 57:15).

We do not lightly claim that the Holy Spirit can and does live within us. This is a gift before which all others pale into insignificance. It is the greatest gift we could possibly imagine, and the fact is that no other religion has imagined it. It is true that in many pagan religions, there is the belief that some god or demon can take possession of a person and live in that person. But in all cases, it is less than the great Creator God of the whole universe, even if they believed in such a God above all gods. For example, the Greek philosophers believed in a great God above all the other gods, but they could not believe that such a god could care about human beings or about anything on this earth. They believed that the supreme god was one who never did anything but sit and meditate on himself. They reasoned that if he did anything, then that showed that he was not absolute perfection. If he thought about anything outside himself, that would show that he did not know everything. If he ever changed his position, that would prove that he was not in the perfect position. So they believed in a strange Supreme Being who could do nothing and certainly could not love anything or anyone.

Outside Christian revelation, no one has dared think of such a thing as the Creator of all things living within human beings, not to get them to do something for him, but because of his love for them. Yet that is what it means for us to receive the gracious gift of the indwelling Holy Spirit. God loves us so much that he wants to live with us and in us and to keep us with him forever and ever. God loves us in such a way that he will never let us cease to be, and he wants us with him always.

It is the indwelling presence of the Holy Spirit, our personal Helper, that makes life with God such a wonderful adventure. We can never be alone, for he is with us always. We may go through things that are very hard for us and have difficult tasks to perform, but this abiding presence of the Holy Spirit makes everything bearable. Even pain and sorrow can be borne when we know that he is there, and that he cares.

We are holy because of his presence, and because we belong to him. We can avoid sin because of his presence and help. We can find our way through dark, difficult places because of his guidance. We can do whatever God desires, because his Holy Spirit is with us to strengthen us and to give us the abilities we cannot have in our own strength.

To know all this is to find in life with God a constant adventure of love. We never know what we will face in the future, or even the next moment, but we know that he knows and that he can take us through it safely. He can even use our troubles to make of us what he chooses for us to be. So there is no reason for us ever to be afraid of what may happen to us. We are often afraid, but this fear is a natural human reaction to trouble and can make us more alert and careful if it does not get out of control. This natural emotion of fear, if coupled with true faith in God and determination to live for him in spite of everything, can put some flavor of excitement into the adventure of holiness. We can be sure of the help of God and of our ultimate victory and need not feel the shaky, paralyzing fear we would otherwise have in the face of danger. And the longer we live for God under the guidance of the Holy Spirit, the more we can trust in his care for us. When we can look back on the many victories he has given us, we can base our present confidence on the sure knowledge of all that he has already done for us. Then the adventure takes on new zest.

So the great gift of the Spirit is the Spirit himself, and this is a greater gift than we usually feel. But that is not the end of the giving by God. Paul speaks of "spiritual gifts" given to us by the Holy Spirit, so it is important for us to come to some understanding of these "gifts."

Gifts of the Spirit

The only extended discussion of the "gifts of the Spirit" is in First Corinthians 12. Like the other topics in this letter, the gifts are discussed because of the troubles caused by the false understanding of them by the Corinthian Christians. In the first chapter, Paul discussed the unity of the church because of the disunity in the Corinthian church. In the second chapter he discussed spiritual wisdom because the Corinthians argued over who of them had the most of it. In chapter 5, he spoke of immorality because the church had been condoning it in a leader. He then writes about lawsuits, because some of the Corinthians were suing others in the church. The discussion of marriage and divorce in the seventh chapter was motivated by distortions of the subject by some of the Christians. Next he wrote about the eating of meat because some of the Christians were disfellowshiping others over their disagreements on the matter. In the eleventh chapter, Paul discusses worship because the Corinthians were hindering worship by some of their habits. For example, they claimed to be partaking of the Lord's Supper when they gathered for a feast. Some who had plenty of food feasted on it, while others who had nothing went hungry. This was a mockery of Christian worship, as Paul made plain to them.

Now, in chapter 12, Paul turns to the matter of the gifts of the Spirit, on which the Corinthians were so divided. They made so much of the more spectacular gift that they sought for what they called "tongues" and neglected to seek for what would build up the church. They were emphasizing what would exalt the individual instead of what would exalt Christ, glorify God, and strengthen others. They felt that those who could speak words that could not be understood by others were more spiritual than those who could not do this.

In response to the situation in Corinth, Paul began by putting the gifts in proper perspective and showing their purpose. He then points out the value of the love of God which is given by the Spirit and then speaks directly to the point of the "tongues" which seemed to mean so much to the Corinthians.

Given to the Church

Paul indicated clearly that the gifts are given to the church, not to the individual Christian. "To each is given the manifestation of the Spirit for the common good" (1 Cor. 12:7). It is for the good of the church that the gifts are given to the individual Christians, not for the good of the individual to whom a gift is given. "And God has appointed in the church first apostles, second prophets" (v. 28). The Holy Spirit appoints these persons in the church. That is, he does not give us spiritual abilities for our own good, but for the good of the church. "Strive to excel in building up the church" (14:12). Paul makes this even more explicit in Ephesians 4:11-12:

> And his gifts were that some should be apostles, some prophets, some evangelists, some pastors and teachers, to equip the saints for the work of ministry, for building up the body of Christ.

So the Holy Spirit gives the gifts to the church, for the good of the church. We must never forget this, because it would lead to a distortion of the purpose of God. When we pipe gas into the furnace and light it, we are not seeking to warm up the furnace so that the furnace will feel better. We are seeking to use the furnace to warm up the whole building. When we send electricity through a light bulb, we are not seeking to light up the bulb, but to use the bulb to light up the whole room. The furnace and bulb are only instruments for the good of the people. The heat and light are not for the benefit of the instruments, but for our benefit. In the same way, the gifts are given, not to individuals for their benefit, but to the church, for the benefit of the whole. This is one of the main points of the chapter.

Many Gifts from One Spirit

Five lists of spiritual gifts are given in the New Testament, and a total of twenty gifts are listed. Each list is different from the others, showing that there is not a set list of things that the Spirit can do through people. Instead, at any set time, the Spirit does what is needed through the persons who are present and ready to be used. This fact is even more striking when we see that three of these lists are in the same chapter (1 Cor. 12), yet no two of them are exactly alike.

Yet all of the gifts have the same source. As Paul says repeatedly, the gifts are different, but they all come from the same Holy Spirit. The unity of the church is assured by the unity of the Spirit who puts it together and works in it.

For just as the body is one and has many members, and all the members of the body, though many, are one body, so it is with Christ. . . . Now you are the body of Christ and individually members of it (v. 12, 27).

Furthermore, the equal validity of all the gifts is assured by the fact that the same Holy Spirit gives all of them. In every case, it is the same Holy Spirit who is working all things in all the people (v. 6). "All these are inspired by one and the same Spirit, who apportions to each one individually as he wills" (v. 11).

Now there are varieties of gifts, but the same Spirit; and

there are varieties of service, but the same Lord; and there are varieties of working, but it is the same God who inspires them all in every one. To each is given the manifestation of the Spirit for the common good (v. 4-7).

All of the gifts are equally valid. No one is to be exalted above the others, since all are useful in the church. Whatever God does in and through us, he does for the good of the church, and he knows what he is doing. He does not work in us needlessly or carelessly. He knows how to build up the church by working in us as individuals. He knows how to use each of us to accomplish in the whole church just what he desires.

There is no reason for us to tell God what to do in us. He knows just what to do and how to do it. If he chooses to use us in a prominent position or in one that seems useless to us, it is not our business to complain or to seek for a higher position. Our business is to submit gladly to his will for us and do what we can where we are in the church. Only in this way can we be of service to God. Whatever we do that is to glorify ourselves cannot truly glorify God. Our work must be to exalt Christ, not ourselves.

It is not by accident that Paul's prose-poem on love is found between the discussion of the Spirit in the Church, and that of the abuse of the gift of languages. Love for the church, which binds the individuals together in the church, supersedes every form of spiritual individualism. Paul's constant emphasis is on the fact that our first desire should be to build up and strengthen the church. Herman Ridderbos, the great Dutch student of Pauline theology, in writing on "love" in Paul's thought, stresses Paul's way of writing against individualism:

On the one hand there is mention here of what the church has received in its several members by way of spiritual gifts; on the other hand of the danger that the principle of self-direction and individualism is strengthened in this diversity of charismata. Paul now deals firmly with this, especially in 1 Corinthians 12 and 13. Nowhere does love emerge more clearly than here in its character as binding together and involving the church. We have Paul's struggle against spiritual individualism in the Christian church to thank for the celebrated chapters, 1 Corinthians 12 and 13.[1]

This does not take away from the importance of the individual persons, or from the variety of the contributions each can make to the church as a whole. But it is the church that is important, not the individual alone. The importance of the individual is seen in his or her contribution to the whole. God loves me, but the fellowship of the Christians is more important and valuable than I am. So I cannot afford to seek my own pleasure, but the good of the church. "Love does not insist on its own way" (1 Cor. 13:5). Love seeks for the good of the church and the glory of God.

The Gifts Listed

The Bible gives five lists of spiritual charismata: Romans 12:4-6, 1 Corinthians 12:8-10; 12:28; 12:29-30; Ephesians 4:11. Each list is different. Since no two of the lists are alike, one wonders how many Paul would have listed if he had written about them in one more place. One gets the impression that the Holy Spirit simply qualifies and empowers each person to do the task at hand, whatever it might be. There is then no set list of gifts. The Holy Spirit can do in and through each of us just what is needed, even if it is something that has never been done before. Those writers are unscriptural, then, who speak of the "nine gifts of the Spirit." They do this by looking at one list only. Yet Paul listed nineteen or twenty. (The total number depends on whether we count them in the original Greek, where we find twenty, or in one of the common English versions, which usually gives nineteen.)

Not all of these are referred to as "gifts" (charismata) in Paul's writings. For example, the Bible never speaks of a "gift of tongues." And we must understand that the Greek word charisma does not mean just the same as the English word *gift.* The Greek word used by Paul puts the stress on the fact that the grace of God is working in the person to help the church. The English word seems to be used to mean that one has been born with a special talent or ability. When we say that one has a gift for speaking, meaning that from childhood the person has been more fluent in speaking than the average. This is not at all what Paul had in mind. He writes not of innate abilities, but of special working of the grace of God in the person through the Holy Spirit, to do the will of God in the church. It cannot be overemphasized that the *charismata* are not natural abilities, but the working of God's grace in the individual Christian. They are not necessarily permanent. If one backslides, for instance, she or he loses both the saving grace of God in Christ Jesus and the special grace of God in the Holy Spirit by whom she or he was enabled to work in the kingdom of God.

1. *Prophecy.* This is the only gift that is in all five lists. It refers to preaching, the proclamation of God's truth under the anointing of the Spirit. The Greek word *(prophemi)* means "speaking for" someone. The prophet speaks for God by declaring the gospel. Contrary to popular thought, prediction is not a necessary part of prophecy. The Old Testament prophets predicted the coming of Christ and his kingdom, and those events that helped prepare the nation for Christ. But the New Testament prophets, like the New Testament itself, looks back to Christ and proclaims his message and its meaning. The essential aspect of the work of the prophet is preaching the word of God in the power of the Holy Spirit. Prophecy is in all the lists and is emphasized by Paul because it is the means by which the gospel is given to others.

2. *Teaching.* Teaching is found in four of the five lists. It is the essential work of instructing people in the meaning of the Bible. Twenty-four times in the Gospels, Jesus is described as a teacher. Paul, in his missionary work, spent much of his time in teaching. Every preacher and teacher needs to have the help of the Holy Spirit in teaching. Some are better at it than others, but each has to do the best she or he can with the ability God has given.

3. *Apostle.* In the New Testament the word *apostle* is applied chiefly to the Twelve and to Paul, who were not only preachers of the gospel, but independent witnesses to Christ in his earthly ministry. They were the pioneer missionaries of the gospel. In this strict sense, there could never be any others. In any case, they performed their ministry in the power of the Spirit, by whom they had been chosen.

4. *Miracles.*

5. *Healings.* Each of these are in three lists and are closely related. The lists are of people through whom God has chosen to bring healing to the sick and to perform other miracles of mercy. God is able to work in and through some Christians in a special way. Healing can be miraculous, but so can many other works of God be called miracles.

6. *Tongues.* Meaning *languages.* Two lists are given in almost consecutive verses (1 Cor. 12:28, 30). Verse 31 explicitly states that all do not speak in tongues. It is clear from the only description of this work (Acts 2:4-11) that it means speaking in a recognizable human language that one has not learned but that can be easily understood by one who knows that language. If I were to speak in Swahili, it would have to be by the help of the Holy Spirit. But I have students who speak it as their native language. If they heard me speaking in Swahili, they would understand me clearly. But that is not necessary, since they also speak English. We shall consider this in more detail later.

7. *Interpreting.* This as well as all the remaining gifts are only in one list. This is the anointing of the Spirit in the translation of what is spoken in another language. Anyone who has preached through an interpreter knows that it is one thing for the interpreter to have an understanding of both languages and quite another for the interpreter to be able to translate both accurately and effectively from one language to another. At such a time, one prays for a God-given, Spirit-filled interpreter. Without such a one, the best-preached sermon can be rendered ineffective.

8. *Distinguishing between spirits.* Every Christian ought to be able to distinguish between good and evil spirits in people. Yet some are enabled by the Spirit to see more clearly and

quickly that a person is not what he or she seems to be or claims to be. This is a valuable gift.

9. *Utterance of wisdom.* It is one thing to know what to say and quite another to be able to speak the right words of wisdom at the right time. In my experience, Elsie Egermeier (known for her Bible storybook) was one who had this gift. But she did not feel that it was a gift, since she worked and prayed to find just the right thing to say to others to help them.

10. *Word of knowledge.* This gift is closely related to teaching and is also closely related to wisdom. But knowledge tends to imply that the person has studied and researched to learn what she or he now says. Yet some have much knowledge without being able to express it clearly in words. This is the gift of God.

11. *Faith.* All Christians have faith as the gift of God, since it is a prerequisite to salvation. But to some is given special faith to trust even when others have given up.

12. *Helping.* No gift can be more needed than the gift of helping others in the kingdom of God. Blessed is the church in which one or more Christians have the gift of helping. It may seem more desirable to be the big worker, but every worker must have many helpers.

13. *Administrators.* Many want to be leaders, but no one can be a leader if she or he has no followers. Some are better at planning and administering plans than others. Some can inspire others to follow their leadership. The Spirit gives some few a gift of leadership that is sorely needed. The worst problems arise because of some who are determined to be leaders and seeks to put down all other leadership in order to rise to the top. This is not a gift, but a sin.

14. *Evangelism.* This Greek word simply means telling the gospel to those who need to hear it. It may mean preaching to vast crowds, but it may also mean a quiet witness over the back fence or across the lunch table.

15. *Pastor.* The Greek word literally means *shepherd.* The great pastor may be a good preacher or may not be. But the pastor knows how to help the people in his or her care. He

or she knows how to feed them good spiritual food, to encourage them to do the work of God, and to give them spiritual rest.

16. *Serving.* This is closely akin to "helping." Serving the needs of others requires true humility and love, but we all ought to pray for the ability to do it well.

17. *Encouraging.* Some of us remember that Charlie Kissel had the gift of encouraging Christians who were about to give up or felt they could not go on. This gift requires close observation of others, caring enough to see when they need a spiritual lift. What a blessing this can be at the time.

18. *Giving.* I am made to feel ashamed when I see how freely and joyfully some Christians give of themselves to the church and to anyone in need, not only in the giving of money, but of self.

19. *Showing compassion.* The gift of both feeling and showing compassion is one we all need at some time in our life. The Holy Spirit is able to lead certain persons to be especially good at this.

20. *Exhorting.* This is the ability of persuasive appeal. God gives to some the gift of teaching the gospel, to others the gift of effective preaching, and to still others the gift of persuading sinners to do what they ought to do come to Christ. It is also the gift of persuading Christians to move forward in their life and work for God.

Probably over the centuries, God has given many special gifts that are not in these five lists. The Holy Spirit can enable a Christian to do what needs to be done at that time in the way in which it needs to be effected. New inventions such as radio and television may call for special abilities, but the Holy Spirit is always able to provide them for the church.

Each of these gifts is an enhancement of ordinary human abilities. The Holy Spirit works with what we already have and makes us capable of doing more than we could ever do without him.

Nature of the Gifts

1. *They are given to the church.* As we have said before, the gifts are not given to the individual Christian for his or her

benefit. They are given to the church, for the building up of the body of Christ. This is especially seen in Ephesians 4:11-12.

2. *They are given as God chooses.* "All these are inspired by one and the same Spirit, who apportions to each one individually as he wills" (1 Cor. 12:11). "God arranged the organs in the body, each one of them, as he chose" (v. 18). "And God has appointed in the church . . ." (v. 28). It is good for us to pray for gifts, but it is not proper for us to demand or seek a particular gift. Neither must we seek to manufacture a gift for ourselves. God is Lord and decides just what to give each person. The choice is his, not ours.

3. *There is a variety of gifts.* There is no hint in the Bible that any one congregation ought to have all of the gifts or that one person ought to expect more than one. Some of us may wonder if we have even one. But if the Spirit is given freedom to work in and through us, he will do in us just what he sees best.

Since the gifts occur in such a variety, there is no scriptural support for seeking to receive any particular gift. No one gift makes a person more spiritual or closer to God than another gift. No gift makes one more fit for heaven than those who do not have that gift. No one gift is the proof of the presence of the Holy Spirit or of the approval of God. No gift is the sign that the Holy Spirit is working in us. The proof of the Spirit is the Spirit himself. If he is in us, we know him and he knows us, and that is all the proof we need. It is all we can ever have.

The gifts are varied because many kinds of work are necessary if the church is to be built up and strengthened. This is the purpose of the Holy Spirit in giving them. His objective is not to make us feel good or to assure us of his presence, but to help us build up others. This is not to edify individuals only, but to strengthen the whole church, as it is made up of individual Christians.

One of our problems is that we take the short view instead of the eternal view. If we can study the history of the church for the last two thousand years, we will begin to see how slowly but surely the church has been brought to its present state. More Christians are alive now than at any other time. More preachers are preaching to more sinners than ever before in the history of the world. By means of modern technology one preacher can now preach the gospel to more people than Jesus preached to in his whole earthly ministry. Granted that some are abusing that privilege and preaching something less than the gospel. But it can be done and is being done. We ought to rejoice. God's Holy Spirit is working in the world now to build up the church in ways beyond our comprehension.

Whether my part in the spread of the gospel and the edifying of the church is large or small, I can rejoice that I can have some small part. I personally have come to the time of life when I realize that some phases of my work in the church have come to an end and that I may not have much more time or strength to work at all. There is a strong temptation to feel discouraged that I have done so little and to realize that I must leave to younger people the task I have only begun. Yet I have come to understand that this happens to all of us. We have a short life of service in this world and then must leave the work to others. No one of us can do much, but we must do what God enables us to do and leave the rest to God. It is his church, and he will take good care of it. So we do what we can and trust God to continue the work through others.

4. *There is unity in diversity.* There are a variety of gifts, but they all come from the one Spirit. He works in and through all of us to bring about a heavenly unity in the church. The Holy Spirit works to bind us together in one. As each of us does what he or she can in the Lord, the Spirit builds us up together into one body, the body of Christ (1 Cor. 12:14-27). All of us are necessary if the church is to be what God wills. So none of us should feel more important or less necessary because of the work we are doing, or the abilities we have or do not have.

It is not wise for us to be too introspective about our gifts. To be overly concerned with finding out what gift we have, or what gifts others have or do not have, leads to trouble in the church. It makes us more concerned with analyzing

155

ourselves than with doing the work of God. Let us simply pray and work to fit into the church in a useful way, and let God take care of the final results.

The worst thing we can do is to feel that our gift is not appreciated and not properly used in the church. If we truly have a gift from the Holy Spirit, he will help others to realize that fact and find ways to make use of it. Our task is not to push others out of the way so that we can exercise our gift. Paul did tell us, "Do not quench the Spirit" (1 Thess. 5:19), but he meant that we must not turn the Spirit away when he seeks to teach us or guide us. He did not mean that if we have a gift we must insist on using it in every church service. He may want us to find ways of using it every day. If there are three soloists in a congregation, all three cannot sing in every service. But a good song can be used in a variety of ways to the glory of God on weekdays. The gifts are for the church, and we must find ways of using them to edify the church.

5. *God governs the church.* It is clear from the New Testament that God is in control of the church. This does not mean that his control is absolute, for individuals can so easily get outside the will of God. Yet Jesus built the church in the first place and is continuing to build it according to his plan. Through the work of the Holy Spirit in individuals, he seeks to direct the organization and operation of the church at all times.

(a) *Charismatic government.* This term comes from the Greek word usually translated *gifts*. So it would mean government through spiritual gifts. God places the members in the body (1 Cor. 12:18) where he wants them, by giving them gifts to fit them for those places.

The term *charismatic government* has come to mean a very loose, unplanned, spasmodic form of governing the work and worship of the church. This was common in the early Church of God movement. This can seem very pleasant to those who are used to it, since everyone feels freedom to express himself or herself in any way he or she chooses, but there are problems here that can become very serious, especially as the church grows larger. When all are free to express themselves, there is no control over those who express unchristian attitudes, emotions, and ideas. There is no effective way of preventing false leaders from leading the church astray. There is no perfect way to prevent such problems, but an unstructured group will soon develop a structure of some kind, and it may be a very poor one, with the wrong people in charge.

(b) *How about an autocracy?* Some have seen the dangers in a spasmodic form of organization and have gone to the opposite extreme. A pastor will set himself or herself up as dictator to the congregation and will make all the decisions for them. He or she may import a military-like chain of command concept into the church and instruct the people to believe that God will always speak to them through him or her. God will tell the pastor what he or she wants done, and the pastor will pass on the commands to others. He or she will demand strict obedience, since he is speaking for God.

But there is no hint of this in the New Testament. A congregation must have proper respect for the pastor, so long as he or she lives a godly life deserving of it. Yet we are told to "test the spirits to see whether they are of God; for many false prophets have gone out into the world" (1 John 4:1). There is no such thing as an infallible human leader. Any of us can be mistaken, and all of us are mistaken at times as to the best thing to say or do. There is safety in seeking the counsel of others.

(c) *A democracy.* The church is a theocracy, which means that God governs the church. But he does it by working in the hearts of individuals to lead them to make wiser decisions than they could make alone. Since the Spirit works in and through individual Christians, the proper way to make decisions that affect the whole church is to find a way, through prayerful discussion and voting, to let all the people agree together on what to do. So it is that the church is a theocracy, but from a purely human viewpoint, it looks like a democracy. Each individual Christian prayerfully considers the matter and then votes his or her convictions. The majority rule is most apt to be what God chooses. It is more likely to

157

be God's will than the decision of any one person.

This is how God works in and through all the individual Christians in a church to make the church what God chooses for it to be. The more we learn to let God lead us in our thinking and acting, the more the church will demonstrate the power of God in this world, to bring the world to Christ.

Tongues

In the last few decades, we have heard so much talk about the phenomenon of "speaking in tongues" that it is necessary to say something more about this. Most people who have experienced this feel that it is the clear proof that one has received the Holy Spirit. One recent writer conceded that it is possible to receive the Holy Spirit without speaking in tongues and said that he had known of two persons who had done so! This was not much of a concession. What does the Bible say about the matter?

The New Testament Passages

The only possible reference to tongues in the Gospels is in the doubtful ending of the Book of Mark. "And these signs will accompany those who believe: in my name they will cast out demons; they will speak in new tongues; they will pick up serpents, and if they drink any deadly thing, it will not hurt them; they will lay their hands on the sick, and they will recover" (Mark 16:17-18). Note first that this passage is textually doubtful because it is not in the earliest manuscripts of the New Testament. It is in the longest such passage in the whole New Testament, since the few other doubtful texts contain only a verse or a few words. We would not be wise to build a doctrine on such a passage. But if we did, we would have to admit that five signs are listed here. It is wrong to pick out one of the five and insist that this is the sign that one is filled with the Spirit.

In Acts there are five descriptions of persons being filled or baptized in the Spirit, and in three of them they spoke in tongues: the first time anyone was so baptized, on the Day of Pentecost (Acts 2:1-13); the first time the gospel was preached to Gentiles (10:44-46); and the first time Paul preached to disciples of John the Baptist (19:6). The Bible does not contain further recorded instances.

In writing his first letter to the church in Corinth, Paul condemns the church for a variety of distortions of the gospel and includes the speaking in tongues, which they were using in a way that did not glorify God or build up the church (1 Cor. 12 14). Paul was here dealing with problems that were disturbing the church at Corinth. If this had not been causing division and trouble there, Paul would not have had to mention it at all. The phenomenon is not mentioned in any of the rest of the New Testament.

When we consider the rest of the New Testament, we note that Jesus spoke much about the coming and work of the Holy Spirit but never once mentioned the speaking in tongues in this connection. Neither do we have any record of him speaking in tongues, though if anyone ever had the fullness of the Spirit, he did! Paul wrote a dozen books in which he did not mention this phenomenon. Peter, John, James, and Jude never mentioned it. Surely this is a clue that it is not as essential as some tell us it is.

The True Gift of Tongues

The true gift of tongues involves speaking a real human language one has not learned (Acts 2:4-11). Fifteen languages and dialects are listed in this passage, and those listening in the crowd each heard someone preaching the gospel in the hearer's own native language.

There is no such thing as an unknown language. The word does not occur in any of the New Testament discussions, as is shown by the fact that the standard versions either omit the word or italicize it. Paul insists that every language has a meaning (1 Cor. 14:10). If it does not have a meaning then it is not a language. If it is not understood by someone present, then it has no purpose, for the only purpose of language is communication.

In this century, some commentators on the Bible, under the influence of their "history of religions" theory, have interpreted the speaking in tongues as "ecstatic speaking." The reason for this is that they assume that Christian practices have evolved from pagan practices. And since some of the older Greek religions and others were often characterized by ecstatic speaking, they assume that Christians practiced the same. There is no scriptural support for this and no support for inserting the word *ecstatic* in New Testament translations.

It is true that the Corinthians may have been speaking ecstatically, but the word must not be used carelessly in translations, for to do so would in many instances give the wrong impression. In Acts, it clearly does not fit what happened. But near Corinth was Delphi, where, in the temple of Apollo, a priestess would answer questions in incoherent words. Some believers at the shrine would fall in an ecstasy and utter unintelligible speech, which they took as proof that Apollo or some lesser god had entered into them and lifted them above other humanity. Since the Christians at Corinth were newly converted pagans, it was natural for some of them to carry over into Christianity this same concept and seek to outdo others by "speaking in tongues." In writing to them, Paul did not deny that there was a real speaking in languages by the Holy Spirit, but he did seek to show them that if it was from the Holy Spirit, it would be real languages capable of interpretation, under the control of the speaker, and would be done in an orderly manner. And he said that it cannot edify the church unless it is made to be understood.

Not the Evidence of Holy Spirit Baptism

Not a single passage of Scripture teaches that speaking in tongues always follows the baptism of the Holy Spirit. In only three of the cases in Acts are we told of speaking in tongues. The majority of instances do not mention it.

Paul plainly states that all DO NOT speak in tongues, any more than all partake of any other of the gifts. Joel said that preaching, not tongues, was to follow the pouring out of the Spirit (Joel 2:28). In Acts 2 preaching, not tongues, is emphasized in the chapter. Paul states that prophecy is more valuable than tongues (1 Cor. 14:1). Further, this teaching that tongues is the evidence of the Spirit would make it a sign to believers, but Paul says that it is not (1 Cor. 14:22). A study of the passage he quotes from Isaiah makes his point even stronger.

Paul knows there is such a gift but does nothing to encourage it. It is the least important gift and is always mentioned near the last, if at all. (It appears only in three of the five lists). If exercised, he says it is to be interpreted so as to edify the church. No doubt he allowed speakers from foreign countries to testify or speak in their native languages, but he insisted that it did no good unless this was translated by someone. So Paul points out that speakers can and must control their speaking (14:32) in order to build up the whole church. The Spirit of God never deprives one of his or her reason of choice.

Paul Compares Preaching and Tongues

When Paul compares these two gifts, he insists that preaching is far superior because it builds up the church. Tongues speaking may help the speaker, but preaching helps the church (14:2-3). Tongues leads to confusion and uncertainty, but preaching gives clear directions (14:6-9). Tongues does not contribute to Christian fellowship, but preaching does (14:1-2). Praying in tongues may make one feel inspired, but it adds nothing to his or her understanding of the gospel (14:14-15). So it is that five words of preaching are better than ten thousand words in a language that is not understood by the hearers (14:1-9). Tongues brings on scorn from outsiders, but preaching convicts them of sin (14:22-25). Paul, who himself spoke in more languages than the Corinthian Christians did, declared that in church he sought to speak in the language of the hearers (14:18-19). He clearly spoke Hebrew, Aramaic, Greek, and Latin, and perhaps others. This is one of the things that prepared him for missionary work. Paul urges them to preach, but he does not urge them to seek to speak in tongues (14:3-9).

Sources of Tongues

All normal Christians long for a deeper walk with God and are seeking for every blessing they know God wants to give them. So when a Christian is told that some have received the infilling of the Holy Spirit and have the gift of tongues to prove it, it is natural for a person to wonder if he or she is missing something valuable. This is especially true if such statements come from some respected person. The person then should seek to understand whether or not this phenomenon is caused by God or comes from some other source.

1. It is clear from a variety of studies that the source of tongues can be merely human. Psychologists have long documented such a phenomenon as a common neurotic manifestation. The historical study of Cutten showed that it is not limited to Christianity and is not always connected with any religion at all.[2] Cross-cultural studies have shown that the phenomenon tends to have many similarities to that in Christianity. Indeed, it is hard to see any difference at all. It is found in many religions even before the time of Christ. As we have seen it was a part of the worship at the Delphic Oracle near Corinth, which was a seat of pagan worship of Apollo. It can come about as a result of a deep emotional experience. It can also be worked up by being urged to repeat a word or phrase faster and faster. Anyone can be taught to do it, or almost anyone, if the proper techniques are used and the person is not too resistant to the idea.

2. It is also clear that the source can in some instances be satanic. We know that demons can and do sometimes speak through persons. In certain religions that center around worship of demons, such as Pocomania, tongues speaking is seen as proof of the indwelling of the demon. This is what Paul referred to in 1 Corinthinans 12:1, as he showed that what is said can help identify the source of the speaking. This is also why John said we should test the spirits (1 John 4:1).

3. It is also true that the source may be God, the Holy Spirit. But in that case, it will be accompanied by holiness and love. He will work in an orderly manner and glorify God. The speaking will edify and unify the church. And it will follow the New Testament rules (1 Cor. 14:26-33), which modern tongues speakers seldom do.

If we speak in the Spirit of God, we will speak of God and

glorify him. Even the Spirit does not speak of himself, but of God the Father and the Lord Jesus Christ (John 14:12-14).

It may help to conclude this brief discussion with a statement from Wilber T. Dayton taken from an unpublished paper:

> But when all is said and done, the New Testament recognizes languages and commands us not to forbid them. Yet it does not suggest that they should be sought. If one observed all of the cautions of 1 Corinthians 12-14, had no motive of self-seeking or pride, and were fully yielded to the discretion of the Holy Spirit in the distribution of gifts, such "tongues" as would remain would edify the saints and would lead none astray. . . . Judging from Scripture and history, this approach would keep tongues at a minimum in the church. The general rule seems to be that where they are not sought they are not experienced. And, besides, what can tongues add to one who already has the fullness of the Spirit? The Spirit himself bears witness. The important thing is to be sure that we have the fullness of the Spirit that is promised in Acts 2. Having Him, vitally, consciously, and dynamically, we can safely let the Holy Spirit himself choose the manifestations. It is not always a holy generation that seeks after a sign. We have a deeper assurance.

Chapter 13:
Fruit of the Spirit

In the midst of his discussion of the gifts of the Spirit in 1
Corinthians 12:14, Paul made it clear in chapter 13 that
the fruit of the Spirit is far more important than the gifts. If
we have all the power of the Holy Spirit but none of the love
of God that he seeks to give, then we are nothing. Of course,
it is no doubt impossible for us to have the gifts without the
fruit, but Paul speaks in this way in order to show the
relative importance.

This discussion of the fruit of the Spirit must, of course,
be a study of Galatians 5:22-23:

> But the fruit of the Spirit is love, joy, peace, patience,
> kindness, goodness, faithfulness, gentleness, self-control;
> against such there is no law.

The fruit of the Spirit means the results of the Holy Spirit
dwelling within us in fulfillment of John 14:16. If the Holy
Spirit lives in us long, we are bound to find ourselves bearing
the fruit of his work in us more and more. He makes us grow
more and more like Christ in our attitudes, actions, emotions
and general character. This is bearing the fruit of the Spirit.

The fruit of the Spirit is the direct opposite of the works
of the flesh, which Paul had listed in verses 19-21. So the
Christian can be distinguished from the sinner by what he or
she is and does.

The works of the flesh are manifold and divisive, while the fruit of the Spirit is single and unifying. Too much cannot be built on the form of the word *fruit* or the word *is*, since the word *fruit* can be either singular or plural, and the Greek words are also somewhat ambiguous. Yet we can see that sin always leads to sins, divides the personality, and tends to separate the person from others. In the same way the fruit of the Spirit is all of a piece, tends to unite the total personality of the person, and builds bridges of love toward other persons. This can be seen even more as we look at each fruit in the list.

1. *Love.* Love is mentioned first because it is most important and because it is the key to all the others. The love of God as described in the Bible is something new in the world and is totally beyond any emotion or way of acting that non-Christians can give to the word.

Christian love is seen primarily in the cross. "Greater love has no man than this, that a man lay down his life for his friends" (John 15:13). Jesus said this on the evening before he was crucified for the sin of the world. "While we were still weak at the right time Christ died for the ungodly. Why, one will hardly die for a righteous man—though perhaps for a good man one will dare even to die. But God shows his love for us in that while we were yet sinners Christ died for us" (Rom. 5:6-8). Then Pauls commands us: "And walk in love, as Christ loved us and gave himself up for us, a fragrant offering and sacrifice to God" (Eph. 5:2). "We love, because he first loved us" (1 John 4:19).

Christian love, therefore is learned from God. He has loved us so much that we can love others in return, as soon as we have come to trust in that love for our salvation. After he has loved us so much, and in such an unprecedented manner, how can we fail to love others? We love God, and we love others, because God has first loved us.

More than that, Jesus said that the mark of the Christian is love for one another. "By this all men will know that you are my disciples, if you have love for one another" (John 13:35). This Christian love is of such a different character from that of the world that it causes Christians to stand out like bright

166

lights in this sin-darkened world.

Christian love is enduring, self-motivated, self-effacing, firm, hopeful, persevering, and redemptive. If we are truly Christian, we love others because God loves both us and them. We love sinners because we were sinners until we were redeemed by God's love in Christ Jesus, and we seek to bring them to Christ for the same salvation we have found. Our love for sinners causes us to treat them redemptively in spite of their sin. We may despise the way they live, but we love what God can make of them. If we truly love them, we will not let their sin turn us away but will seek to free them from their sins by showing them the Redeemer.

Christian love is the fruit of the Spirit. "God's love has been poured into our hearts through the Holy Spirit which has been given to us" (Rom. 5:5). Probably there is no more important statement in the Bible than this about the work of the Spirit. It is more important for us to have the love of God poured into our hearts than to have all the power of the Spirit to perform mighty miracles (1 Cor. 13:2). It is more important to have God's love in our hearts and to manifest it, than to speak all "the tongues of men even of angels" (1 Cor. 13:1, author's translation). The love of God in the heart is more valuable than all the sacrificial deeds we might perform for others without it (1 Cor. 13:2).

So the Spirit works to pour the love of God into our hearts. The fruit of his work within us is the growing love for God for other Christians, and for sinners.

John Wesley always insisted that holiness can best be described by calling it perfect love. This is no doubt true, since holiness is the love relationship of a person with the holy God. We may speak of "perfect love," since love can be perfect without being mature. The love of a child can be perfect love though capable of years of maturing. The maturing of love is the goal of Christian growth in the Spirit and is the result of the work of the Spirit subsequent to sanctification. It is the work for which salvation and sanctification prepared the way. Perfect, mature love is the goal and crown of the Christian life of growth in the Spirit.

167

2. *Joy* Christian joy is inseparable from godly love and impossible without it. Joy springs from a life that is gracious, kind, and loving. Real joy grows out of love for God and love for all human beings. So Christian joy is not based on circumstances, but on the relationship of the soul with God.

The word *joy* occurs sixty times in the New Testament and the word *rejoice* seventy-four times. It is not so because Christians had it easy all the time, because they did not. The Book of Philippians, which was written from prison, is built on the theme of rejoicing in the Lord. Lying in prison for the sake of the gospel, suffering as a criminal though he was not one, Paul could write to others to tell them to rejoice. The joy he had was not based on circumstances but on his relationship with God.

We can have joy in the Lord that transcends all troubles and circumstances. This joy comes not from our circumstances, but from God through the work of the Holy Spirit within us. For that reason the outward characteristic that most distinguishes Christians is their constant joy. It is not the kind of artificial smile that has to be pasted on before going out, but rather the joy that wells up from within.

Christian joy is the joy of being forgiven by God. After living in sin, and then coming under the convicting power of the Holy Spirit, it is a source of real joy to know that God has forgiven and accepted the sinner. To know the love of God gives joy that nothing can take away.

Christians have the joy of trusting in God. There is no reason to worry and fret about what might happen, for we know that God will take care of us. We know that we do worry at times, but when we come to God in prayer, if we have learned to trust in him, we realize that our worries are needless and fruitless. Then our trust can be renewed and our joy restored.

We have the joy of Christian fellowship. We love all human beings in the Lord, but a special joy comes from fellowship with other Christians that nothing else can match. That is one reason we love to go to church services. We love to be with other Christian friends. Many of us who have unsaved loved ones have found that our Christian friends give us a kind of fellowship we can never have with unsaved relatives. What a blessing it is to be with people who love God just as we do and who love to talk about the things of God. It is with them that we can grow in our love for God and for one another.

We have the joy of working for God, knowing that our work for him can never be in vain, whether we ourselves see the results or not. It is a source of joy just to know that what we are doing is for the Lord who loves us. To be doing his will is our only great desire. So when we are working for him, we are doing what we really want to do more than anything else in the world. Who could not have joy in this kind of work?

There is joy even in affliction, since we know for sure that God will reward us in the end if we are faithful to him. No matter how much we suffer in this world, we know that it will not last forever and that God will go with us all the way. He knows what it is to suffer and is able to sympathize with us in our own affliction. And he is able to carry us through it all with victory and joy in our souls. We live in his presence here in this world, whether suffering or not, and are eager to have in eternity the kind of unending fellowship with him that he has promised us. Even when we come to the point of death, we know that he will go with us through it and that we will find ourselves after death in face-to-face fellowship with him forever.

There is the joy of witnessing for Christ. As we seek to bring others to Christ, we find a special joy in soul-winning that cannot be known any other way. To see another person receive the joy of salvation is something the Christian can never forget. The only thing that can surpass this is the joy of helping that new Christian friend grow in the grace and knowledge of the Lord. We know that if that person will remain true to God, as we are seeking to do, we can rejoice together in heaven in the joy of having helped one another to get there.

The greatest joy of all is the joy of anticipating eternity with Christ. It has become unfashionable to talk about heaven, but we must not yield to this fad. Jesus taught us to rejoice in the fact that our names are written in heaven (Luke 10:20). The hope of heaven with our Savior is enough to carry us through all the troubles and tribulations of this earth with great, unquenchable joy. "Just one glimpse of him in heaven will the toils of life repay." It is heaven on earth just to feel the presence of the Lord with us. What will eternity with him be like? An old saint exclaimed to me, "I can hardly wait to see what God has prepared for us there!"

3. *Peace*. The ancient Greek ideal was to get peace through getting rid of all desires. They believed that one could have real peace in his or her heart if he or she got rid of all emotion, stifled all desire, and became totally self-sufficient, so that he or she did not have to be dependent on anyone for anything.

The Christian concept of peace is far different. The Old Testament word for peace meant not the absence of conflict, but positive well-being, or the state of being truly blessed by God.

The normal Hebrew greeting was *shalom*—peace, and among the Christians "peace" was a standard greeting, used with the Greek "grace." Paul often used both: "Grace and peace." But he usually added that both grace and peace come from God through our Lord Jesus Christ. Over and over both Jesus and Paul prayed that we might have peace, so that the word occurs eighty-eight times in the New Testament.

Christian peace is peace with God, first of all. In Christ we have a new relationship with God that transforms the whole life into one of peace. Only as we have peace with God can we have peace within our own souls and peace with others. If we have made peace with God, as we have been reconciled to him in Christ Jesus, only then can we have peace within and true peace with others, whether Christians or sinners. When we have this kind of God-given peace, we can develop peace within the church, which is the ideal that God would have us reach.

The point of Paul's list is that peace, like the other virtues listed here, cannot be worked up in our own strength, but has to be given us by God through the Holy Spirit. Furthermore, the peace we would like to have may not come to us suddenly but has to have time to grow and mature. The Holy Spirit can cause this peace to grow in our minds and hearts. Yet it is miraculous what the Holy Spirit can do at times when sudden trouble comes upon us. He can instantly give us the calm peace in our souls that carries us through the emergency so that we can only look back later and wonder how we kept so calm. This is the work of the Holy Spirit. And yet the slow growth that takes place over the years is also the work of the Spirit and is just as miraculous. The sunflower that shoots up so quickly is no more miraculous than the giant sequoia that grows for centuries. It is all the work of God.

4. *Patience.* The Greek word used here is an interesting one, and one that can only with difficulty be put in a single English word. It is the opposite of "short-tempered." So it means that one is patient in enduring trouble and oposition. It is bearing with the weakness of others. It is suffering without retaliation. It is imitating the patient kindness of God. Just as God has borne with us in all our sinful rebellion until we finally turned from sin and came to him, so we should learn to be patient in all our dealings with others. But this patience with sinners is purposeful. We want to help them, and we want most of all to help them find peace with God. We are patient with other Christians because God has been so patient with us, and we want to help others grow in grace along with us.

If we take an honest look at ourselves frequently, we will have less difficulty being patient with others. God has put up with so much in the best of us that we ought to tolerate much in others. If we remember how God saved us from sin, even when we did not at all deserve it, we will find it easier to be patient with those who are still far from salvation.

5. *Kindness.* This is sometimes translated *goodness or gentleness.* It is a beautiful word for a beautiful fruit of the Spirit. The Greek word is quite similar to "Christ" but is not really related to it. Yet it is so true that to be Christlike is to be gentle and kind. This Christian kindness is a manifestation of

godly love to others. To treat others gently is to treat them as God has treated us. It is easy to fight back when we are hurt, but it takes a growing maturity in the love of God to be gentle with those who are hurting us. How we need to pray for more of this fruit in our lives!

6. *Goodness.* The Christian must not only be good, but good for something. The true goodness of the Christian is like a beacon shining out in a dark world of sinful night. It shows others the way to the One who gives us his goodness. It makes us worthy of his call and calling. It demonstrates divine love.

An evil spirit has grown in America that makes us afraid of being called good, as though we are afraid that being good is being boastful. The world describes it to us in these terms and says that anyone who is good is being "holier than thou." But this is simply not true. God is good, and if we are to be like him in any way at all, we must seek to be truly good.

Young Christians especially face the kind of pressure from peers to go with them in their evil ways. The Christian youth is made to feel that the only way to gain the respect of others is to give up the desire to be good and act as they are acting. What we need to realize at such a time as this is that these persons are convicted of their own sins by the goodness of Christians. If they are to find any peace in their own souls without giving in to God, they must either give up their own sins or try to drag Christians down to their own level. Christian goodness is a powerful force for God in the hearts of sinners.

7. *Faithfulness.* Faith and faithfulness can be the same word in the Greek, but probably Paul was here stressing the idea of faithfulness, or, as Barclay suggests, loyalty. To be faithful is to be like God, for God never will forsake us or change his nature. God will always be the same in his love and concern for us. Even if we persist so long in sin that death intervenes, and he has to be the judge who condemns us eternally, it will not be because he has ceased to love us, but because we have lived our lives in such a way that he had no alternative. He has given us free will to choose how we

172

shall live, and he has no choice but to let us take the consequences of our life-long choice.

We need a growing loyalty toward God that will hold us steady in all the temptations and trials of life. Whether young or old, we need to settle our hearts in loyalty to God so that nothing can move us from that determination to be true.

We need to be loyal to God's people, the church. Most of us would easily criticize the church if we just let ourselves do so. There is always much that we can find to condemn in the church. For one thing, no church can be perfect so long as you and I are in it! As a pastor, I used to wish I could find a church with no problems, but deep down in my heart I felt that if I did find such, they would not let me have anything to do with it. Seriously, no congregation can ever be perfect in this world, because if it is growing as it should be, then new sinners will always be coming into the services. Indeed, that is the only way a congregation can grow. Some will always come to church for some of the wrong reasons. All of these can cause problems in a congregation and can give us much to condemn. We may then be tempted to leave the church. But, like Peter, we ought to realize that there is no place to go. To leave the church would be to leave the best group on earth.

Besides that, we need a growing love for God and for his people that will make us stay with the church and work for it, no matter what may be going wrong. Of course, if every person in the congregation backslides and becomes a vicious sinner, then we would have to decide whether there was still a church there or not. But that is not what usually happens. Churches differ and find fault with one another and some-times even split over very small things. I have seen two church leaders almost come to blows over a detail of decoration in the sanctuary! I knew of a congregation that split into two congregations over the matter of eating in the church. All agreed that that was all right. A question arose when someone brought a teakettle into the church building to heat water, and others thought that was sinful! Quarrels often come over the little matters, not over the matters of eternal importance. We need to develop more loyalty to the church that will keep us from being so critical and quarrelsome. The harmony and unity of the church is more important than our proving ourselves right. If we will seek first of all to build up the church, we will come to see that we ourselves are not all that important.

(8) *Gentleness.* The KJV says "meekness," which is a good word, but it has changed its meaning so much that it probably gives most English speaking people the opposite meaning from that intended by Paul. It gives most of us the concept of a doormat type of person, which is not at all what is meant. The Greek word, like the one that follows, signifies inner strength that is so self-assured that one can be gentle and kind with others. The meek person does not fight back at persecutors, not because he or she is weak-willed, but because he or she is so sure of his or her rightness before God that he or she is willing to be mistreated since he or she knows that God and right will win in the end.

Gentleness is a beautiful word for a beautiful virtue in any human person. Note the way Paul uses the same word a few verses after this: "Brethren, if a man is overtaken in any trespass, you who are spiritual should restore him in a spirit of gentleness" (Gal. 6:1). The meaning is emphasized when we note that the word translated "restore" is one that was used by Greek physicians of setting a broken bone. It must be done firmly, but with gentleness, so that the bone will be able to grow together with no further damage being done to the person. Otherwise the doctor might compound the fracture and cause permanent damage.

In our work with others, whether sinners or Christians, we need to learn how to be more gentle with them. Just as we are easily hurt, so are they. We have tender feelings, and so do they. We often need tender loving care, and so do they. We can be so concerned with our own feelings and our own problems that we are brusque or even harsh with others, much more than we intend to be. This is why we need to learn to listen to the Holy Spirit as he prods us to change for the better. Some people may be born with more inclination

174

to be gentle than others, but if gentleness is a gift of the Spirit, then surely prayerful obedience will make us more Christlike in this grace.

9. *Self-control.* The KJV lists "temperance," but this word has come to change its meaning to a very narrow one. Self-control is closer to the Greek word, which literally means "inner strength." So it means "controlling self through God-given inner strength." It is purposeful self-control. We control ourselves for the purpose of glorifying God and making the work of God possible. We control our actions in order to give God a chance to control our lives. We discipline ourselves in order to follow closely the leadership of the Holy Spirit. How we need to grow this fruit!

Characteristics of Fruit-Growing

Fruit-growing takes time. We should not expect either ourselves or others to be bearing mature fruit of the Spirit the moment they are saved and sanctified. For a tree to bear fruit, it must first come to a certain maturity itself and that takes time. Some trees bear fruit the first year, but most take from two years up to begin to bear fruit.

We should always be more patient with others in this matter of the time it takes to bear fruit than we are with ourselves. We must insist on working hard to bear all the fruit of the Spirit as possible, yet we must be very slow to condemn another who does not bear the kind of fruit we think suitable. We do not know the conditions under which the other person is struggling. That person may be giving all her or his energy just to keeping alive spiritually. Another may be having temptations or tribulations we know nothing about, so that it is not easy to grow quickly. We must be patient and let God work.

Fruit requires cultivation. The Spirit works within us cultivating spiritual fruit, but we need to learn how to cooperate with the Spirit. If we know what he is trying to do in us, we can more helpfully work with him to bring forth the kind of fruit he desires. Fruit cannot be forced to grow, but it can be helped. As water, cultivation, and fertilizing can aid the growth of fruit on a tree, so prayer, Bible study, faithfulness in church, and meditation can aid in growing the fruit of the Spirit.

No two grow fruit just alike. What we mean here is that no two of us are alike in our ability to grow fruit. We may seem to have the same time and opportunities to bear fruit, but there may be vast differences. A tree may fail to bear well because of a huge hidden rock hindering its growth. One may have weaknesses or problems that others do not recognize. We have no right to judge the Lord's servants too critically. He will do the judging at the proper time and with infinite love, wisdom, and justice. What we need to do is make sure of our own faithfulness.

The Holy Spirit produces the fruit. We can never force ourselves to bear the fruit of the Spirit, but we must wait on the Lord. The indwelling Spirit produces the spiritual fruit in us. We can and must work with him, but he must cause the fruit to grow. It is only by abiding in him, and he in us, that we can bear any fruit at all.

Fruitbearing requires pruning. Even after our total commitment of our saved lives to God for entire sanctification, pruning must be done, and God will do it if we let him (John 15:2). Some things must be removed even though they are not at all sinful, in order that we may bear more fruit. Bearing the spiritual fruit of love and all the rest is more important and valuable than all the pleasures that we might justify as not sinful. We have to give up even good things if we are to have the best. Just as one may prune off perfectly good blossoms and branches in order to let all the strength flow into what is left, so God may want us to give up some perfectly good things in order to bear more of the fruit he needs in us.

The Ethics of Holiness

The ethics of holiness is seen in the fruit of the Spirit. Here we begin to see what holiness does to the life and work of a person who has been saved. Just to read the list of the fruit of the Spirit is to see that the Christ is living by new ideals and is seeking to measure up to new standards.

As Christians we can never be satisfied with knowing that

we feel different inside. We know that our living must be different or our inner feelings are meaningless. When the Spirit takes up his abode in the heart, we are "sanctified wholly" in relation to God, but this inner transformation must work itself out in a new life-style that must be constantly growing more Christlike. One of the great passages on this is Philippians 2:12-13:

> Therefore, my beloved, as you have always obeyed, so now, not only as in my presence but much more in my absence, work out your own salvation with fear and trembling; for God is at work in you, both to will and to work for his good pleasure.

When we are told to "work out" our own salvation, we can be sure that Paul is not telling us to save ourselves by our works, for that is what he spent so much time in several books to show impossible. No. He is telling us that after we are saved, we must work hard at growing the kind of spiritual fruit that will make us more and more pleasing to God. We cannot cause the fruit to grow, but we can do the cultivating that will help it grow. And we can consciously work with God, who is working in us to do his own will in us. God is at work within us, so we can work also and know for sure that our labor will not be in vain.

What we need to work at is developing and cultivating the spiritual virtues that God is seeking through the Holy Spirit to grow within us. These fruits of the Spirit determine the kind of ethical decisions we will make, and the kind of actions that will ensue.

The ethical failures that cause Christians to lose out are not usually caused by lack of proper academic training in ethics, but by a neglect of the life of the Spirit. When a genuinely converted Christian backslides, it is usually not because she sat down and carefully thought about how to make the right kind of ethical decision but then made the wrong decision because of faulty logic. It is usually because she did not spend enough time cultivating the fruit of the Spirit. Or, he neglected the prayer, Bible study, and meditation that would cause the fruit to grow. He spent too much time on doing and not enough on being.

All of this goes counter to much of what we are hearing today. We commonly hear that we ought to get out of our churches and out of our prayer closets and go out into the real world where sinners need to hear about Jesus. And there is truth in that. If we spend all our time in church, we will almost never win anyone to Christ, because most sinners will never come into the church building. But we are not in danger of doing quite that. If we spent all our time being concerned with our own salvation and holiness, we would never go to others. But that is not our problem today. What we need to hear is the warning that we need to spend more time cultivating our life in God so that we will grow the fruit of the Spirit. In that way we can lift up Christ to the world of sin, and he will draw people to himself. It is not a matter of either/or: either work to cultivate the fruit of the Spirit in ourselves or win others to Christ. We cannot do the latter unless we first do the former. Unless we cultivate our own spiritual strength we will have nothing to give to others. So we must "work out" our own salvation "with fear and trembling" before God, so that we will be able to lead and attract others to Christ for salvation.

As we work, we must never forget that only the Holy Spirit can cause the fruit to grow. We can never do it in and of ourselves. Yet we must not sit down and wait for the fruit to grow or for God to do all the work. We must work because God is at work in us. God is working in us, both to help us know what he desires and to help us achieve his ends. Our work for him will not be in vain, for he is working with us. Knowing that gives us hope and courage to keep on doing our best. If he is with us, what have we to fear? If he keeps his approval on us, we can go on in trust and hope that God will eventually make of us something good and useful even if we do not always feel good or useful. God has never demanded that we be successful in all we attempt, but only that we keep on doing our best to do his will. Leave the results to him.

Peter urged on us this very work in similar terms:

For this very reason make every effort to supplement your faith with virtue, and virtue with knowledge, and knowledge with self-control, and self-control with steadfastness, and steadfastness with godliness, and godliness with brotherly affection, and brotherly affection with love. For if these things are yours and abound, they keep you from being ineffective or unfruitful in the knowledge of our Lord Jesus Christ.

Chapter 14:
The Eternal Adventure

Eight times in the New Testament, Christianity is called "The Way." It was called this even before the followers of Jesus were ever called Christians. It is a good name for the way of Christ. Christianity is not really a "state of being" but a way of living and growing in Christ. We enter the Christian gate on a certain date and every day after that determinedly walk in the Christian way. It is not so important to know that we were converted ten years ago, as to know that we are right now walking in the way of Christ. The beginning of the Christian life is only the beginning. It is the continuing and ending that really count eternally.

Back in the days when railroad passenger travel was the most common way to take a long trip, I sometimes heard salvation compared to a train that goes to heaven. They said that you get on the train when you are converted, and you must stay on the train until you get to heaven. But that is not a good way of describing what really happens, since that would make it all too automatic and easy after the first effort of being saved.

Holiness is not a train you get on, but a trail you must walk on. You get on the trail when you are converted, and you continue to walk in the way all the rest of your life. The trail leads through valleys and over mountains, across rivers and over deserts, through beautiful places and into hard ways. But you keep on walking on the way with Jesus by our side, and the Holy Spirit within.

The Way of Holiness

The way of holiness is the Christian way of believing and the way of living. Christians do not believe the same as others or live like others. We march to a different drummer, as though we belong to a different world. We are in the world, but not of it. "Our commonwealth is in heaven" (Phil. 3:20). We live in this world, but our permanent citizenship is in heaven. So we live differently, and we think differently. In our thinking we use the same kind of logic as the best of other thinkers, but we often come to different conclusions because we begin with different premises. In our living we work with different sets of values, so we have heavenly goals. Thus our actions are different from those whose highest values are purely earthly and temporal.

A Way of Believing

The Christian way is the way of *believing in God the Father, Creator of all that is, and Sustainer of the universe.* He not only made all things, but is continuing to hold all things together. To believe in God is to believe that he is all-important. Our lives are in his hands. Our all is loaned to us for a while by God. When we read that the worker cried out to Elisha when his axe had fallen into the river, "Alas, my master! It was borrowed" (2 Kings 6:5), we realize that all that we have is borrowed and that we have no eternal claim to anything in this world. The hours of the day are loaned to us, and when they are gone, we can never have them back. Our houses, cars, clothes, books, and our very lives themselves are all borrowed for a short period of unknown duration. Before long we will have to give them all back and can keep nothing whatever.

Only one life; 'twill soon be past.
Only what's done for Christ will last.

What we believe about God and eternity does make our life what it is. We should never imagine that it does not matter what we believe. Either we believe in God and what he tells us of eternity, or we are left to imagine that this life is all that there is.

The way of holiness is a way of *believing in human beings as made in the image of God*, and therefore capable of being saved from sin and made like God. Human beings are not utterly different from God, or we could never know God or love him. We are finite, while God is infinite. We are small, while God is greater than the whole universe. But we are made in such a way that we can seek after God and find him. We can know God and talk with him. We can know and do his will, and we can love him wholeheartedly.

The way of *believing is the way of accepting that sin is contrary to God's will*. Sin is a fact of existence in the world, but not a necessary fact. God permits sin, but sin is not a part of the plan of God, for we were made for a higher purpose. Nevertheless, God mades us in such a way that we can choose the wrong as well as the right. So human beings have sinned and cut themselves off from God.

There is no isolation so great or so terrible as when persons sin and tear themselves away from God to do their own evil will. Sin is not just a mistake of no real consequence. Sin is a terrible rebellion against God that robs us of the presence and power of God and cuts us off from our Creator. This is the Christian way of believing about sin, and it sets the Christian off from those who minimize sin.

The way of holiness is the way of *believing in Jesus Christ as Savior and Lord*. When we have sinned, we need forgiveness from above. We have gotten ourselves into a dilemma from which we cannot escape. We need someone outside of ourselves to pick us up from our own mess and set us on the way of holiness and help us to walk in it. No one can do this for the sinner but God in Christ Jesus. The Holy Spirit is the minister of salvation.

The way of holiness is the way of *believing in the Holy Spirit* as guide and helper. Jesus promised another helper, the Holy Spirit, who is sometimes called the Spirit of God, and sometimes the Spirit of Jesus. Jesus gives us the abiding presence of the Holy Spirit to go with us all the way through life and death, into eternity.

The way of holiness is the way of *believing in the church as God's people*. The decision to become a Christian is an individual one. But once this decision has been made, we become one with all other Christians everywhere, who have also made that decision. There is then a unity, love, and fellowship in the church that can never be found outside it. We love one another and we love God and know that God loves us. The Christian way is the way of believing in the church as God's own people.

The way of holiness is the way of *believing in life after death*. Fear of death is very common. If we cannot face up to life, we cannot face up to death. Or to put it differently, we are not ready to live until we are ready to die. If life is all in all to you, then death is the end of all. In that case, death is horrible beyond words and the end of all existence and meaning. But this is not the Christian way.

The way of holiness is the way of *believing in life after death*, because of the resurrection God has promised. God, who made our bodies and souls, will know how to raise us up after we die, and then we will die no more but live on with him forever. This way of believing in death changes the whole outlook on life. When we know that death is not the end of everything, we know that eternal values are more weighty than temporal goods. We know that this temporary life is good and important, but that it is only the preparation time for the life to come. So we do not lay up treasures on earth, for such treasures will vanish away. But we lay up for ourselves eternal spiritual treasures in heaven.

The Way of Living

Holiness is the way of *living victorious over sin*. There is no other way under heaven to have victory over sin. But in Christ we can have that very kind of victory for which the world longs so deeply. There can be no holiness without victory over sin, because sin is the very opposite of holiness. So the way of holiness is the way of true victory in Christ. We can and will be sorely tempted yet need not yield to temptation. We can keep our faith in God and our trust in the Holy Spirit to guide us and help us so that we will be able to stand against all evil and live for God. This victory over sin through faith in God makes life a joyous adventure and gives one real happiness and peace, even in the midst of troubles and tribulations.

Holiness is the way of living *with a disciplined body, mind, and conscience.* The best things in life are not really free. Anything that is worth much has a high price. If you want a beautiful tree, you must learn to prune it, sometimes cutting off perfectly good branches and leaves, so that the whole may grow and shape itself as you want it. That is the price of growing that tree. If you would live a beautiful life of holiness, you must pay the price. You must learn to prune off many things in your life. First you must dig out all desires, habits, and actions that are displeasing to God or harmful to others and cut them off mercilessly. You must get rid of all that will hurt you or others, or keep you from loving God with all your heart.

But there is more. As you work at your Christian life, you will find that many things are not evil in themselves but only keep you from doing all the good you want to do. You may find, for instance, that reading the morning paper is not sinful but that you may need to spend less time with it in order to read the Bible or to have a less hurried devotional period with the family. You may find that you have to give up some favorite television watching in order to have time to commune with God and with loved ones.

We do more or less what we want to do. We all have the same amount of time. If we want to find time for our families and for God, then we will. If we want to do certain work for God in the church, we will make time to do it. If we want to have more time to contribute to the life and well-being of the family, we will make time for this. In the process, we will find ourselves leaving off good things, in order to make way for better things. This is the secret of people who have time and energy for the things that really matter. Discipline makes the difference.

Paul spoke of this when he compared the way of holiness to competition in athletics (1 Cor. 9:24-27). Just as the athlete exercises self-control in what she or he allows, the one who seeks to walk in the way of holiness forces himself or herself to leave off what is less important or what would hinder her or his development and growth, so that what one does is done as well as possible. All strength and energy must be concentrated on what is important. This is discipline and it is the only way to perfect holiness. We must train our bodies, minds, and souls in the way of holiness. And this training is unending. We can never give it up.

The way of holiness is the way of *facing trouble with faith and hope*. The Christian way of facing trouble is a new and different way. If our faith is firm in God, we know that God loves us and we love God. Our hope is God. We know that wherever we go and whatever may happen to us, God is with us. We do not know what will happen to us, but we know who is with us. His grace is sufficient for us.

The way of holiness is the way of *dealing with temptation with decision and grace*. We must struggle if we are to be always victorious over sin, because temptations will come to all of us as long as we live. Even Jesus was tempted. Hebrews says that Jesus was tempted in all the ways we are tempted (Heb. 4:15). But he was victorious over all temptation and promises us that we can be victorious also.

Indecision makes temptation more severe. If we are not really sure what we want to do and what kind of life we want to live, if we have no worthy goals or aims, temptation will find us an easy prey, and we will fall. But if we have truly made up our minds and know what we want to do, if we know that we want to live for God alone, then that decision itself makes it easier for us to say no to any temptation and mean it. God can give the victory when we firmly decide to reject temptation and call on God to help us overcome. God gives victory that brings real joy in deliverance. Then we can look back on the trial and say with the psalmist:

But as for me, my feet had almost stumbled, my steps had well nigh slipped. . . . But for me it is good to be near God; I have made the Lord God my refuge, that I may tell of all thy works (Ps. 73:2, 28).

Besides our decision and God's grace, our love to God and to others helps us overcome. We love God so much that we would not do anything to separate ourselves from him in any way. We love others so much that we would not willingly do anything to hurt them either (Rom. 13:10).

The way of holiness is the way of *meeting death as another adventure*. The Christian way of meeting death is unique. The Christian funeral is not like others. As the Christian faces life with faith and hope, she or he comes to the end of this life knowing that the same Holy Spirit who has been with him or her all the days of her or his living will be with her or him just the same in dying. She or he knows that death is not the end of all, but only an entrance to fuller life. The grave is not a dead-end street but a gateway into eternity. We look forward to the future life eagerly, though we hate to leave the friends of this life. We know that we will soon be reunited with all of them, and then there will be no more sorrow, no more parting, no more grief, and no more pain. God shall wipe away all tears, and we will have joy forevermore.

So the sorrow of leaving loved ones is softened by the sure knowledge that we will be with Christ on the other side of the door called death. We do not know what it is like on the other side, but we know that it is good, for God made it. Facing death with no deep fear, we can face life with real courage and confidence.

The life of holiness is a life of adventure. We can face it as we face any other adventure with hope and confidence, because we have a sure guide who will go with us all the way. The adventure of holiness is unending. It demands from each of us our wholehearted commitment.

Notes

Chapter 3

1. N. H. Snaith, *The Distinctive Ideas of the Old Testament*, 1944, 24ff.

2. C. E. Brown, *A New Approach to Sanctification* (Anderson, Ind.: Gospel Trumpet, November 6, 1954).

Chapter 5

1. Richard S. Taylor, *A Right Conception of Sin* (Beacon Hill Press, 1945) 9.

2. Ludwig Kohler, *Old Testament Theology*, trans. A. S. Todd (Philadelphia: Westminster Press, 1957) 170.

3. James Barr, *The Semantics of Bilical Language* (Oxford University Press, 1961) 233-34.

4. Moises Silva, *Biblical Words and Their Meaning: An Introduction to Lexical Semantics* (Grand Rapids: Zondervan, 1983) 28.

5. Gustav Aulen, *Faith of the Christian Church* (Muhlenberg Press, 1948) 228.

6. A. H. Strong, *Systematic Theology* (Fleming H. Revell, 1907) 549.

7. Merne Harris and Richard Taylor, "The Dual Nature of Sin," in Kenneth Geiger, ed., *The Word and the Doctrine*, 92.

8. William B. Pope, *A Compendium of Christian Theology* (Wesleyan Methodist Book Room, 1880) 29.

Chapter 6

1. G. C. Berkouwer, *Studies in Dogmatics: Sin,* (Grand Rapids: Eerdmans, 1971) 14.

2. John Wesley, *Works,* X (Grand Rapids, Mich.: Baker Books) 223.

3. H. Orton Wiley, *Christian Theology,* Vol. II (Beacon Hill Press) 123.

4. C. E. Brown, *The Meaning of Sanctification* (Anderson, Ind.: Warner Press, 1958) 99.

5. W. T. Purkiser, Richard S. Taylor, and Willard H. Taylor, *God, Man, and Salvation* (Kansas City, Mo.: Beacon Hill Press, 1977) 86.

6. H. Bavinch, *Gereformeerde Dogmatick* 79, quoted in English Berkouwer, 445.

7. Richard Taylor, 112.

8. W. O. E. Oesterley, *The Psalms* (London: SPCK, 1955) 274.

9. Wilbur Dayton, *Wesleyan Bible Commentary,* vol. 5, 38.

10. William Temple, *Nature, Man and God,* 367.

Chapter 7

1. George Allen Turner, *The Vision Which Transforms* (Kansas City, Mo.: Beacon Hill Press, 1964) 51.

Chapter 8

1. J. Sidlow Baxter, *A New Call to Holiness* (Grand Rapids: Zondervan, 1967) 73-88.

2. C. W. Naylor.

3. John Wesley, "Christian Perfection," *Works*, VI, 167-68.

4. Thomas Cook, *New Testament Holiness* (Christian Literature Crusade, n.d.) 19.

Chapter 10

1. George Allen Turner, *The Vision Which Transforms* (Kansas City, Mo.: Beacon Hill Press, 1964) 120-21.

2. Charles W. Carter, ed., *A Contemporary Wesleyan Theology* (Grand Rapids: Zondervan, 1983) vol. 1, 529.

3. H. C. Moule, *Veni Creator: Thoughts on the Person and Work of the Holy Spirit of Promise.* Quoted by William Greathouse, "Full Salvation and its Concomitants: in Kenneth Geiger, *The Word and the Doctrine* (Kansas City, Mo.: Beacon Hill Press, 1965) 218.

4. W. B. Pope, *A Compendium of Christian Theology* (Hunt and Eaton, n.d.) vol. 3, 28.

Chapter 11

1. John Wesley, *Works* vol. 11, 430.

Chapter 12

1. Herman Ridderbos, *Paul: An Outline of His Theology*, John Richard De Witt, trans. (Grand Rapids: Eerdmans, 1975) 295.

2. George Barton Cutten, *Speaking with Tongues, Historically and Psychologically Considered* (New Haven: Yale University Press, 1927).

CPSIA information can be obtained at www.ICGtesting.com
Printed in the USA
LVOW10s0902240916

506048LV00004B/8/P